AND NOW MY SON,
WHEN YOUR FAITH IS CHALLENGED

LETTERS FROM A FATHER TO HIS SON REGARDING AN
EVIDENCE-BASED, LOGICAL APPROACH TO ANSWER
SECULAR ATTACKS ON CHRISTIANITY

Stephen F. Johnsen, Ph.D.

sfjohnsen@gmail.com

TABLE OF CONTENTS

ACKNOWLEDGMENTS

When I look back on books I have read, I found I always skipped the Acknowledgments as they were, to me, boring statements of appreciation to people I did not know. I realize the reader will have a similar response, but now that I have gone through the toil and loneliness one can feel when writing, I have come to appreciate the time and effort people have gone to in my behalf. They did it out of the goodness of their hearts and in considerate support of me. It is a strong message how people of goodwill are willing to go to considerable personal inconvenience in helping another person and do it expecting no reward. This is love, Christianity in action.

First mention goes to my wife, Dale, who engineered the format and, in spite of many demands upon her time, spent uncountable hours twice going over the entire initial manuscript line-by-line, word-by-word with me. I find I have some good ideas but am extremely inefficient in putting them into words others can appreciate. Dale has provided a spiritual influence in the writing and has been invaluable in helping me with this. I am so fortunate to have her love and dedication.

I would like to thank Charlie Burnett, an attorney and good friend. Charlie not only read and critiqued my very first effort, a 250 single spaced page ponderous accumulation of loosely organized, awkwardly written notes, but then had the moral strength to accept a second reading of the current iteration as it was developing. His comments, concrete suggestions, encouragement, thoughts, and stalwart friendship have been invaluable.

I would like to thank Eric, one of my sons, who very patiently also read that first version and made many comments and corrections. Much of what he provided gave me the direction to re-format in present form. My son, Adam, who has tolerated many hours of hearing various points and commenting with informed information upon them. My son Allen, who has also patiently tolerated repeated comments. My son, Michael who introduced me to an atheistic book that had some effect on my formulation in this book. John Williams, old college friend and retired Chemistry teacher suggested a change that was a core element in this version.

The Schaerr family whose invaluable encouragement I received provided the impetus for the undertaking of this version of the book. The time Dr. Val Hemming, took to read and make constructive comments of the initial book. Val, a physician, longtime family friend, is a gifted intellect and very busy man. His comments were instrumental in the eventual formatting of this version. Linda Fields, highly accomplished organist with a journalistic background, took time from a brief vacation to make some pertinent comments.

Another significant help was Dr. Michael Peterson, dentist and good friend. Mike has stood with me throughout the writing of this version of the book, lending moral support, providing many suggestions and helping with wording. Mike has done this in spite of times of considerable personal pressure, stopping to take the time to respond. He is a gifted writer and I hope someday we see something from his pen.

While we were spending a few months in an unfamiliar town, I gave a rough draft of an iteration of the current book to a member of our Church as I thought it would help answer a question she had that related to a specific section. Norma Larsen read the draft and provided very valuable feedback that was the final impetus to rewrite in the current form. Norma, a published author, demonstrated real courage and love in her comments.

Shirley Cox, Sociologist a good friend and very busy person who spends considerable time giving service to others, has been immensely valuable in both providing exceptional emotional support but helping find channels to get this manuscript into publication. In full disclosure, I must admit I introduced a "discreetly packaged" bribe of several Salted Nut Rolls but it was after considerable help from her and she did not solicit it.

Finally, Katie Brooks who interrupted a very busy and pressured schedule to help edit this version. Katie has provided the expertise, intellect, spiritual guidance, and patience that has been invaluable.

Importantly, while these individuals have all played a part in the production of this book, it should not be assumed they necessarily agree with part or all of what is said. Their support was unconditional.

If the reader has considered these acknowledgements, I think it will be a reminder of the help others give us and the love they are willing to share. May you be as fortunate in thinking about this and experiencing it, as was I.

FORWARD

President Boyd K. Packer warned the youth in 2011 when he said, "You young people are being raised in enemy territory". → *the adversary is everywhere*

As our Christian youth, their parents, and all of the faithful are being bombarded with secular thinking and ideals there are loud voices designed to not only discourage active participation in religious practice but to ridicule it. These voices are undercurrents that are receiving increased influence in the world society.

only the gospel of Jesus Christ can adequately hinder Satan's arm.

We arm our children by teaching them the gospel. We teach them to pray we teach them to feel the Spirit. We encourage our children to read and ponder the scriptures and to build their own testimonies. We encourage church attendance and other wholesome activities so that they will keep the goals they have set for missions and temple attendance. At the same time, many of the world's authoritative voices are shouting opposite principles. Some of our youth have only a fragile testimony and are feeling confused and losing the sensitivity to the Spirit as a result.   Many of faith have chosen to ignore the issues; possibly because they do not have the information they need to combat the assaults.

Faith in the Lord Jesus Christ

It is often during the years of academia a person is most at risk because of the constant assault of secular thought. It creates a perfect storm as this is usually the same time that our children experience natural physical urges and develops an emotional need to separate from their parental teaching. As a result many find it difficult to defend their Christian beliefs, even to themselves. This book is written using logical thought and empirical evidence to make obvious that if minds are open Christianity is not just able to "hold its own" but can be defended, effectively asserted, even in an academic atmosphere.

Admittedly, it is hard in this noisy Internet age, when many people make claims and counter claims, to recognize truth. You can't discern it by the number of voices asserting that something is true. The critics tend to focus on a half empty glass and ignore the half full. You can't take something for reality just because a number of the studies or opinions back it up. You can't count on something just because a persuasive expert purports that it is true. You have to find out for yourself

This is the reason I have spent several years researching the secular arguments about religion and the actual data and evidence that exposes incomplete arguments, distortions and in some cases absolute untruths. This is not a book to promote dissention; it is merely giving explanation through a series of emails between son and father that answer many of the secular arguments. BY using logic and facts we are given logical avenues to follow President Uchtdorf's 2013 counsel to "doubt your doubts". This book acknowledges, using empirical and logical evidence through balanced and respectful language, the half empty glass focused on by critics but also emphasizes the half full, well, maybe three quarters full aspect as well.

I was raised in a Protestant home, my mother was very active teaching Sunday classes and teaching my brother, sister and me. In spite of my mother's efforts, several events began to cause me to challenge religion and even God.

First, being coerced by my parents to attend summer bible school, I was "captured" one day by overly zealous adult leaders during recess, the only activity I was enjoying at the time. We gathered up by the pulpit of the rural church building and they asked me if I was "saved." At ten years old, I didn't know and I didn't care. But before our discussion was over they had me on my knees praying. The other kids in the bible school were outside for recess, looking in the door and viewing all of this. I was confused, humiliated and angry. I decided at that young age that, "If this is what God is like, then I want nothing to do with Him." My mom, being concerned, smoothed it over by getting the representatives at the school to agree they would not repeat this kind of pressure on me, and, over the years, I let it go, or so I thought. What I didn't realize then, however, is that experience may have had an emotional effect on me as I became increasingly cynical toward organized religion and cultivated the opinion that religious people were basically phonies.

The second significant event occurred the summer after my senior year in high school while working in the Black Hills of South Dakota. One day off, I hiked into the wilderness and decided to "test" God by loudly profaning Him. I fully believed that if I did this, I could be struck dead and nobody would ever even know what happened. Somewhat to my surprise, nothing happened. In fact, the memory I have of my impressions afterwards was hearing the songs of the birds and feeling the beautiful warmth of the day. I began to conclude God, if He existed, was irrelevant.

The final event came that year when I left the Black Hills at the end of summer to drive back home (a trip that took around 12 hours). I stayed for a party that evening, anticipating an all-night drive. If I followed a pattern I had developed in the past, I would have prayed in a perfunctory way for a safe trip. This time I thought about the options and outcomes. If I prayed and arrived safely, it would be said, "God protected me." If I prayed and was killed or injured, it would be said, "God meant it to be." If I did not pray at all and was injured or killed, it would also be said, "God meant it that way." I realized, "they" had it covered regardless of the scenario. I decided not to pray. About 3 hours into the trip, I fell asleep at the wheel and rolled the car. I was knocked unconscious and awoke on the roof in the back seat of the overturned car with gas pouring out of the tank. Amazingly, I had no serious injuries. The sheriff in that remote part of South Dakota area told me that I rightly should have been killed in that car accident. The conclusion I drew from these events at the time was that there is no God.

By the time I had completed my Bachelor's degree in Psychology, I was no longer merely indifferent. I had become aggressively hostile to religion and religious practice. At that point, I probably could have accurately said I was an atheist, but since I was unable to actually prove there was no God, I settled instead for agnosticism.

Mom was very diligent in her church service and dedication but she frequently expressed the opinion that the church she was attending was not the actual church Jesus had set up on earth, but it was the best thing she could find. One day, the Mormon (Church of Jesus Christ of Latter-day Saints) missionaries knocked on her door and she invited them in. Almost immediately she responded decisively to their message and was baptized into the Church of Jesus Christ of Latter-day Saints. In sharp contrast, I, along with both my brother and my dad were quite certain by that point that my Mother had totally lost it. The result was a very negative attitude on our part toward the Mormon Church.

By the time I begun to study for my Master's degree in Psychology, I was completely comfortable with my agnostic stance. I no longer questioned my position on religion, or even thought much about it anymore. What happened next was utterly unexpected, and to me, unthinkable, except that it actually happened. One day, while driving home from a visit with friends in New York City, I suddenly had an intensely strong feeling unlike any I had ever had before. Amazingly, but without question, I knew that I should join the Mormon Church. I guess it was what some might call being "born again." The reality of this feeling was so profound, and so far beyond anything I had ever experienced, that I could not simply write it off as some kind of a fleeting emotional reaction.

I had gained some knowledge about the Mormon Church from debating the missionaries upon occasion during their visits to the house, as well as from conversations with mom but, prior to the experience, I didn't even believe in a God, let alone feel a desire to join any organized religion. My conviction as to the reality of this experience caused me to forsake my previous animosity and I joined the Church of Jesus Christ of Latter-day Saints. As a postscript to my crude challenges to the existence of a God (cursing Him in the field and refusing to pray prior to the road trip), instead of receiving no answer, I believe His response was love, patience, and compassion. Regarding my childhood bible school experience, while I continue to find the rhetoric foreign, I have developed an appreciation of some individuals of that orientation.

Shortly after joining the Church, I had to conduct my Master's thesis by "running rats." In order to control for outside distractions, I prepared myself to dig in for several long days in a small room with a lot of down time. Planning ahead, I went to the University library and checked out every book on "Mormons" I could find. As it turned out, I spent an extensive period of time in isolation reading, what turned out to be, anti-Mormon literature. This was the only information I had on a lot of topics relating to the church and so I had to "put on a back burner" several issues that were disturbing and I could not explain. When time allowed, I then set out on a quest of examining some of those issues. The Church taught simply that truth was truth and we should not be afraid of it. As I examined certain issues, I found that much of what I had read was either misinformed, distorted, quoting out of context, setting up "straw men," or even blatant falsehoods.

My first literary endeavor was to write an article relative to the charges that Joseph Smith, the founder of the Church, was hallucinating or engaged in fraudulent claims. My training in Psychology and my research into the life of Joseph Smith allowed me to easily dismiss these charges as uninformed. The article was accepted by the Church's Sunday school *Instructor*, but never published as publication had ceased shortly after.

Many years later, I decided to ask the question, "What empirical evidence is there that Jesus was resurrected?" I purchased books and searched for publications by atheists, pro-Christians, agnostics, skeptics, scholars, and others. I took notes because the issues began to become unexpectedly complex and varied. My first "book" (never published) was an unmanageable text with about 250 single spaced pages. It was boring to read and somewhat difficult to understand due to the extent, variety, and volume of comments. I came to consider it to be more of a reference. I am acutely aware of the extensive and varied current day challenges of religious issues directed to adults and youth. As a result, I felt inspired to write a usable book; a summary of the former notes. I hope this version is more to the liking of many who have not previously examined these issues or want a different perspective on them.

From this study (both pro and con) of literature relative to God, Jesus, the Old Testament, the New Testament, and the Book of Mormon, I arrived at a strong empirical verification of a certain knowledge spiritually that there is a God, Jesus of Nazareth was the predicted Messiah, He was resurrected, and the Book of Mormon is what it claims to be: an actual ancient record and another testament of Jesus Christ.

I have tried to represent the core issues in as few words as possible with a readable form. I have chosen an email format between father and son, in part, because for me it represents a very real situation. I have attempted to fairly represent both pro and con positions, something that is very rare in the material I went through. It is my hope that you, the reader, will find the same excitement, knowledge and satisfaction from this experience that I did.

Finally, the wording, expression of issues, and approaches are my own and do not represent any organizational position including that of the Church of Jesus Christ of Latter-day Saints. The ideas in this book should not be interpreted to be endorsed by any of the people who helped or encouraged the production.

CHAPTER I

RELIGIOUS ISSUES

Dear Dad,

You know, even though I'm not attending a religious school, I didn't realize the topic of religion would come up so frequently. In fact, I didn't realize I would be bombarded with a lot of criticism and questions about my religion. Even the professors are into it. The other day in class, one professor said, "Religion ... relies on the gullibility of its clients, who have been educated to believe without evidence and without explanation."[1] I don't want to fall into that category.

All of my life, I have grown up with a lot of beliefs about my Christian faith that I have never questioned. I have always taken them for granted. Now, all of a sudden, I am getting all kinds of unsettling ideas from friends, literature, the Internet, and from my teachers. These ideas are challenges to and criticism of, not only my "Mormon"[2] beliefs but of Christianity itself. I'm not surprised to find this attitude from atheists but I am surprised that so much of the general public seem to think that Christians are non-thinking, gullible fools. The basic assumption is that Christianity has no concrete, scientific "proof," but is based only on blind and ignorant faith.

Have you ever run into this? I could use a little guidance.

---

[1] Harriet Hall writing a book review for the *Skeptical Inquirer.*

[2] "Mormon" is a nickname given to members of the Church of Jesus Christ of Latter-day Saints (LDS) by people who were hostile to the Church. It originally had an extremely pejorative, demeaning tenor. Over time, however, it seemed to lose some of the hostile intent and is currently commonly used. Mormon is a major figure in the Book of Mormon.

Dear Son,

It's really fun for me to see so much of myself in you. School is meant to challenge you and encourage you to look at and question things. I suspect at this point you are experiencing some confusion between those spiritual truths you were taught throughout your life and the apparent lack of proof. Driven by similar confusion, I have read extensively over the years and I have data points that I think will be of interest to you. We've never had this discussion before because I wanted you to reach a point in your life where you yourself were asking questions; it looks like this is the time.

Before we get into this, keep in mind that faith, a very real concept to those who experience it, is the cornerstone of religious belief. I suspect that to the people whom you are writing about, faith is not an acceptable answer. The issues you bring up are not about religious faith, but rather empirical evidence (observable data) and so this is how I will focus my answers.

Let's start with the statement from your professor that Christians (or religious people in general) are non-thinking, gullible fools, ". . . who have been educated to believe without evidence and without explanation."

During my years as a Psychologist, I have found it helpful to study the complexities of human thinking and how people can be absolutely unaware of the errors in how they arrive at conclusions. The quote you give is an example of someone paying attention only to the information they agree with while ignoring or being unaware of the other available data. In this particular instance, the use of demeaning terms like "gullible" and "fools" is a signal to me that the author is stepping beyond factual data and has some self-protective emotion behind it. Now, to be fair, this phenomenon occurs on both sides of the aisle, from the believers as well as the unbelievers. Many religious apologists,[3] as well as skeptics, do not realize that a considerable amount of empirical or cognitively rational evidence does actually exists. However, they are holding so tightly to their own conclusions, thereby narrowing their field of reality, that they are not able or willing to see anything more.

It seems that in your experiences and what you're lacking is the "evidence and explanation" to answer the criticism and questions you are facing. Son, tell me, what specific questions do you have about this?

Thanks Dad,

It is a real relief that you are able to understand what I am going through.

The more I read, the more confusing things seem. Some of the more severe critics in one of my classes are describing Christianity as a fabricated story and some are even contending Jesus did not exist as a person. They[4] say the physical and divine

---

[3] Apologist is a term used to describe a statement supporting a religious position. I want to make it clear that it is not interpreted as being apologetic.

[4] Earl Doherty (p. 8), a Canadian (atheist?) presents, I think, a well-articulated, and, for the most part, relatively free from emotionally self-defensive strategies (rare for many atheistic writings about Christians) summary of challenges to the validity of Christianity. If you read only Doherty's writings, and don't consider other data, one can be easily swayed to accept his conclusions that the New Testament is a fabrication of mystical ideas. I find his writings a very informative encapsulation of a skeptical viewpoint and, while I strongly disagree with much that is concluded, I must admit, I enjoyed the challenging, thought provoking presentation.

nature of Jesus, was made up around AD 150 to AD 200.[5] Other scholars say that only about 25% of the sayings attributed to Jesus in the New Testament are authentic.[6] They conclude that if the miracles were real, he would have attracted a lot of attention yet there are no sources outside of the New Testament referring to him. Some (such as the *Passover Plot*[7] book) say that He was literally invented or concocted for political purposes. The boldest critics argue Paul was speaking metaphorically. One author often quoted says Mark was "an imaginary writer, whose name we don't know, in a community we're not sure." This unknown author, now called Mark, created a composite Jesus of Nazareth. Mark is considered a source document used by authors we call Mathew, Luke, and John. They ridicule the reality of the resurrection, or the fact that Jesus had any sort of divine or supernatural powers[8]. They say religious people are dealing with cultural traditions that are false. There is no concrete (or what you would call empirical) evidence anywhere. I'm hearing a lot of

---

[5] Until recent years, the dating concepts were AD for at the time of Christ's birth and BC for time periods before Christ's birth. There is a current trend to substitute BCE (before the Common Era) and ACE (After the Common Era). For personal reasons, I choose to retain the BC and AD notation, in part, because they both still refer to the same time periods; Christ's birth.

[6] Robert Funk and the Jesus Seminar. The Jesus Seminar is a body of about 150 scholars from diverse (some not Christian) backgrounds that met annually and voted on which scriptures they considered to be factual and which were made up. Strobel, an apologist quoting Boyd (p. 115-116) states "the Jesus Seminar is as biased as Evangelicals, even more so." The Jesus Seminar tends to reject the validity of any reference to supernatural events.

[7] Controversial 1965 book by Hugh J. Schonfield.

[8] See Wikipedia, Jesus Seminar for detail of one scholarly group's opinions.

criticism challenging the Old and New Testaments as valid sources.

I'm not sure what to think about all of this.

Dear Son,

Boy, you really have been bombarded, haven't you? You may not know this about me but every one of the positions you have just described are ones that I, myself, at one time or another, have subscribed to. Perhaps instead of "subscribed to," it would be more accurate to say, "Forcefully advocated."

There came a point in time, however, when I received a very strong, unexpected and unsolicited personal testimony of the truthfulness of the existence of God and the religious teachings you were brought up with. The testimony was so strong, I could not write it off as a fleeting emotion and it was qualitatively different from any aesthetic or awe inspiring experience I had ever had (or have since had). This began to open my eyes to the reality of religious issues, a reality I had previously been not only unaware of, but also even a little hostile to. As time has gone on, I have become increasingly convinced that my previous views (and those of many current strong critics) about God and Christianity really represent an extreme position in a person's thinking.

Sit tight; we've got a few answers.

A general principle we will encounter several times, in my opinion, truth for any given person is a matter of the information they pay attention to and the importance they give it. Allied to this, it is as important sometimes to pay attention to not only what is said, but also what is not said.

Let me take on one basic question immediately: "The historical figure of Jesus of Nazareth never actually existed at all." If the scriptural references are in doubt and no longer considered a realistic document of history it follows that one would doubt the reality of Jesus of Nazareth. As you mentioned, it is claimed by some that, outside of the scriptures, there is no mention of Jesus as a person prior to AD 100[9], almost 70 years after he was crucified. Well that's not quite true.

A major exception is a reference in Josephus,[10] a first century Jewish/Roman historian, mentioning Jesus in his writings in two places. The critics, however, will note some wording in each of the two references that are not characteristic of Josephus' style. To make matters worse these statements do not appear in earlier versions of his writings. Therefore, critics discount these entire references. On the other hand, the most zealous apologists ignore there is a problem with them. The truth is that if we go back to Josephus' original texts, Jesus is still referred to as a person though his divine nature is not. This is a good example of people only paying attention to the information that agrees with their perspective. It also, however, gives an additional source of the historical existence of Jesus.

Another reference outside of the scriptures is that of Tacitus (AD 55-120) who was a senator and a historian of the Roman Empire. He documents, in his *Annals and the Histories,* Nero's record of Jesus being put to death by Pontius Pilate as well as the Christians "pernicious superstition" surrounding Jesus; this is easily interpreted as the Christian belief in his resurrection.

In addition, there are two more early Roman writers who refer to Jesus as an actual person. Suetonius (AD 70-130) a Roman

---

[9] Doherty, CV p.35

[10] Josephus in *Antiquities of the Jews* mentions Jesus twice. Josephus, a Jew, born around AD 37 (around AD 94) remains a non-Christian source that places existence of Jesus as a real person and is very close in time.

historian who wrote during the early Imperial era of the Roman Empire, mentioned Christians and their leader "Christos."[11] A little later, Lucian of Samosata, (AD 125-180) a Greek satirist wrote of the Christians (although not about Jesus specifically) in a satirical mode.[12]

An additional body of literary works claims some letters of Pilate, and others of prominent leaders of the time, mentioned Jesus but their authenticity is questioned. Kimball (hpc) draws heavily on those documents that are not generally found in discussions such as this. They include existing letters claiming to be written by well-known figures (e.g. Pilate, Herod, etc.). Also used in documents that are considered to be apocalyptic documents such things as Mary, the mother of Jesus, escaping to England at the time of the Roman assault on the Temple in Jerusalem. I am not familiar with the pro and con data regarding them and so I am not including them as evidence. I will say, however, there is a good degree of plausibility that some of the information lends itself to some interesting, if not intriguing, possibilities. As you can see son, there is documentation of Jesus' life and death by non-biblical sources during the first century.

Beyond the historical figure of Jesus, we may also examine events and places as documented in the New Testament to find point of concurrence. You may remember in Mark 15:33 and Luke 23:44 a darkness at the time of the crucifixion is recorded. Two ancient Greek writers, Thallus (AD 52) and Phlegon, who lived in

---

[11] It should be mentioned that scholars note Christos was a common name of the time and Suetonius may have been referring to another person.

[12] Some scholars question how much Suetonius knew about Christians, thus qualifying the veracity of the assumption it refers to an actual historical person.

the second century AD referred to the crucifixion and to the darkness at the time.[13] Again, supporting actual existence of Jesus as well as the recorded events in the Gospels at the time of the crucifixion.

In addition to the Greek and Roman writings, there is some archeological evidence relating to the reality of Jesus as a person. Archeologists have discovered and dated the tomb of Joseph of Arimathea. This was identified because it had been a traditionally maintained location as the tomb where Jesus was placed immediately after the crucifixion. Let me clarify what I mean by "traditionally maintained." In AD 300, Roman Emperor Constantine's mother set about the task of identifying Christian landmarks. She was able to locate the tomb site because of traditions of relatives of Jesus and others identifying the site. Excavation eventually disclosed a tomb that fits the descriptions in the New Testament.

Often cited as strong archaeological evidence is a dwelling in Capernaum, again maintained by tradition. It is believed that this is Peter's house and is characterized by the design that would allow a man to be lowered through the roof into the house (Mark 2:4). Remember Peter was a fisherman by trade. Excavation of a fishhook on the floor of the same dwelling adds some validation. Of course, this is a house found in a fishing village and so a fishhook might be expected in most houses. Also, I honestly don't know if this particular roof design is unique, and so in my opinion this is not as strong as some of the other evidence we will site.

---

[13] McDowell (p.122-123), discusses Thallus (AD 52) and Phlegon (a second century Greek historian) as secular authors mentioning the darkness. Thalius explained the phenomena as an eclipse but McDowell points out Paschal (the time of darkness) was during the full moon and so a solar eclipse could not have occurred.

While it does not seem to be frequently mentioned, I consider a third site to have some validity, the tomb where Lazarus was reportedly raised by Jesus (John 11). This site located near Bethany, like the tomb of Jesus, seemed to have been carried over the years by tradition. Coins were found on the tomb floor dated at the time of Jesus.[14]

A more recent archeological find is an ossuary, a stone box where the bones of a deceased person were placed after the flesh had rotted off. This box dates to the time of Christ. The inscription on the box identified the contents as, "James, brother of Jesus." While both names were common to the culture, the occurrence of the two names together significantly reduces the probability of the names being just random occurrences. There has been a long court battle over the issue of the person who owned this box having forged the "brother of Jesus." A final legal judgment determined the owner did not forge the contested inscription. I am aware that some hold the opinion it was possibly forged by someone else. To further complicate the issue is the actual name of Jesus' brother was most likely Jacob[15]. I am not certain how James got into the picture and tends to throw authentication further into question. It is just really hard to validate something this old. I came across a study regarding a recent excavation in Nazareth that is focusing on a house, believed to be that of

---

[14] Finegan (p. 159). As a matter of tangential interest is a second tomb identified as that of Lazarus, but the second could well have been the tomb of Lazarus' final resting place.

[15] Madsen, Truman interview with ancient biblical language expert David Noel Freedman

Jesus.[16] Confirmation is yet to come but it just goes to show this work of empirical evidence is ongoing.

Regarding the concern you posed, that Jesus was "created" for political or theoretical purposes, you bring up the argument made by some that Paul, in his references to Jesus, was speaking metaphorically and did not consider Jesus to be a real person. Remember, Paul never personally met Jesus unless you conclude he had some direct experience through his vision at the time of conversion (and, of course, the critics do not accept this). He did report having talked with people who had seen and known Jesus. This gets into differences by scholars over the translation of some terms used by Paul. The disputed words have several options for translation ranging from receiving the information about Jesus through inspiration (critics) versus receiving the information from the reports of individuals who knew Jesus (apologists). If you would like to see more discussion on this, I have attached a discussion (Appendix A).[17]

Remember that the empirical and logical addresses only a limited portion of the issues. It ignores the importance of the spiritual aspects. To a person of spiritual faith it is as real as the

---

[16] Ellen White cited in an internet article from the March/April 2015 issue of Biblical Archaeology Review (BAR). The house is close to a well in the town where tradition (non-canonized James, Wikipedia) & (NIV Luke 1:20-33) says Mary received the vision from the Angel Gabriel that she was to be the mother of Jesus (Annunciation).

[17] Doherty (Challenging) (p. 62) for example, focuses on Paul and on the word "paralambo" having the most appropriate translation referring to visionary experiences, thus not referring to Jesus as an actual person. Doherty (Jesus Puzzle) (p. 71) also mentions the use of the term "ophthe" as referring to simple visions. Jones, (p. 91-92) takes issue arguing the most appropriate alternative interpretation or "paralambo" refers to information obtained by Paul when he interviewed Peter, Jesus' disciple.

empirical. I believe truth is best found when both are used together.

Dad,

I understand about the spiritual aspects but it's difficult to explain that element to those who are only willing to look at empirical evidence. At this point, those are the people I feel I'm really battling. I always thought science is objective and yet I find even people who insist on dealing only with scientific evidence can become so emotional.

Son,

I'm guessing from your note that you are perhaps having some pretty heated discussions. May I caution you to try to pull yourself away from this? Contention is not a good, or productive, forum for truth seeking. Remember, truth for any given person is the information they pay attention to and the importance they give it. Watch for what is not said as well as what is said.

I have come to the conclusion that people, even those who focus on logical thinking, can sometimes have personal, or emotionally self-defensive reasons why they reject the existence of God. These may be reasons that they are themselves completely unaware of. This phenomenon can occur even though their reasons for rejecting them are not entirely rational. While in our discussions, you and I have been focusing on skeptics; people of faith can be caught up in the same issues. I've attached more on these thoughts in a note if you are interested (Appendix B).

When we consider the empirical evidence of the history (the information that we currently have) of Judeo-Christianity it can be understood why a person might develop doubts. Doubts are sometimes what drive us to discover truth. However, when we react to an idea that is threatening to our own set of assumptions, we may no longer be in truth-seeking mode. Instead, we may take emotionally defensive positions. This is when anger begins to dominate and logic becomes distorted. If we can recognize our own feelings on this and make attempts to maintain civility and respect, honest discussions can occur. In my opinion real faith and also the pursuit of real knowledge means we should never be afraid of truth.

Dear Dad,

I'm sure you are right, Dad, but sometimes it gets really hard, especially that bit about maintaining civility and respect in an emotional discussion.

Here's another question for you that has come up in my own study of the topic: Is it true that the scriptural stories weren't written down until around the middle of the second century? If this is true, how can we be sure they are real events?

Son,

It is true that we have no original source documents of these events. The first reference to written documents that we currently have was by Justin Martyr around AD 160. They were referred to as *Memoirs of the Apostles*, thought to have been written before Justin's time. It is believed the original teachings of Jesus were transmitted orally and may, or may not, have been written down. The people of the time were basically illiterate and any written documentation had to be done by the hand of a learned person. Those who were learned tended to be primarily the wealthy.

Though some scholars do refer to literate Christians who were recording gospel events, the absence of written records is not a strong support for questioning the validity of events. At the time, memorizing scripture was the primary focus of Jewish religious instruction. In fact, this is still true in some Jewish and Muslim traditions. The accuracy of what was learned became paramount. Verbal transmission of information, particularly religious teachings, was likely much more accurate than would be found in today's society. Eventually written documentation became more prevalent but over time as the writings were translated and copied, variations in views resulted.

Dear Dad,

Funny you should mention variations in the written text. I've recently been reading about the Nicene councils. What's the deal with that? I had the idea the early Christian doctrine was pretty well understood and agreed upon by all. I am now learning there was strong disagreement and even conflict between different Christian groups.[18] Did Emperor Constantine order the Nicene Council to stop the fighting? That's kind of what I get from my reading. Do you know what this is all of this about?

Dear Son,

The Apostles, set apart by Jesus and representing the authority of leadership, were eventually killed off while isolated in separate locations. The process for replacing an apostle was for

---

[18] Ehrman (p. 173) quotes Bauer, "Orthodoxy and Heresy in Early Christianity" as noting early (pre fourth century), ...as far back as we can trace our sources, could be found a number of divergent forms, none of which represented the clear and powerful majority of believers against all others. In some regions of ancient Christendom what became labeled as 'heresy' was in fact the earliest and principle form of Christianity."

the remaining apostles to meet and appoint a successor. [19] Obviously because of their isolated condition, this became impossible. This is what the Church of Jesus Christ of Latter-day Saints considers to be the beginning of the great apostasy, or the beginning of when the authority to govern the church established by Christ was lost. The Roman Catholic Church believes Peter, the leading apostle, appointed a successor, eventually descending to the present day Pope.[20] This is where the process of authoritative leadership became a matter of disagreement between different Christian groups.[21]

As early Christians began to collect writings and documents, some authors were selective (for example, only using the letters of the Apostle Paul), others were creative in the writings.[22] You are right, one of the tasks of the Nicene Council was to specify what writings would be acceptable for official use in the church and put a cease to disputations.

---

[19] Acts 1:23-36 provides a commonly referred to reference of the process of the replacement of apostles.

[20] Kimball & Stirland note evidence a number of early Christians fled to England and formed a church structure separate from the Roman Church.

[21] Ehrman (p. 193) notes other Christian groups also claimed a direct lineage of their teachings back to the apostles. Valentinus was claimed to be a disciple of Theudas who was allegedly a follower of Paul. The Gnostic Christian Basilides studied under Galukia, a supposed disciple of Peter.

[22] According to Kimball & Stirland, scholars have identified thousands of documents that were at various times and places accepted as legitimate sources. Kimball (and Kimball and Stirland) draw from the "Apocrypha" and other ancient documents along with the canonized scriptures to provide some interesting and thought provoking possibilities of the details related to Jesus and those associated with him; accounts covering his life between birth and the final years.

Divergence of opinion seemed to be the rule since the death of the apostles. There were major contentions that Emperor Constantine wanted to quiet. One if the major points of argument brought to the Nicene Council had to do with the nature of the Godhead. Some of today's Christian churches might be surprised to learn that major disputes arose over the idea of God the Father, Jesus the Son, and the Holy Ghost being three separate entities.[23] It is important to recognize Constantine financially and materially supported the Roman Christian religious leaders' thinking of the time. Eventually, through the Nicene Council this was settled, unsatisfactorily to some, by stating the Father, Son, and Holy Ghost were distinct, yet are one substance, essence or nature, called the Holy Trinity.[24] (See Appendix C for a more detailed discussion.)

Even after the Nicene Council, further divisions in thinking continued. As you may know, in the early 1400's Martin Luther, a Roman Catholic monk, raised public objections to some of the practices of the Church that he considered to be corrupt (e.g. the granting of papal indulgences). He was imprisoned and excommunicated but attracted followers who established what eventually became known as the Lutheran Church. Others such as John Calvin, began to raise additional issues, and further churches began to be formed. All of these broke from the Roman Catholic Church becoming known as Protestants. Since they broke from the claimed authority line (from Peter) of the Roman Catholic

---

[23] A 2014 Christmas movie with an Evangelical slant touted St. Nicholas (Santa Claus) as physically assaulting people who advocated God, the Father, Jesus, and the Holy Ghost were actually separate entities.

[24] Wikipedia, Holy Trinity, paraphrased.

Church,[25] they generally tended to reject the concept of formal ecclesiastical authority.[26] Some of these fought among themselves over their doctrinal issues, sometimes becoming violent.[27] Some of our atheist friends use these as well as other acts of violence to support their claim that religion is the source of most wars, though this is hardly a Christian position.

A very limited number of examples of some of the evolving groups that we recognize today are: Baptists, (originating in the 17th century by John Wycliffe during the Protestant reformation focusing on baptism of adult members by total immersion), Methodists, separating from the Church of England (emphasizing personal relationship with God), Seventh-day Adventists (focused on Saturday for the Sabbath), Christian Scientists (directing focus on metaphysical healing), Mennonite and Amish (concerned with issues regarding infant baptism), and one group called the Shakers, or Shaking Quakers (focused on celibacy and became extinct).

As a personal aside, while there have been disagreements and scandals within the Roman Catholic Church, I think this church has done a good job of preserving core concepts and the image of Christianity throughout the world over hundreds of

---

[25] Kimball (p. 20), notes the succession to authority took a long time with Popes first being elected in the sixth century.

[26] Kimball (p 20), notes prior to the Popes, the political regional bishops were the ecclesiastic ruling council at the time. Kimball also notes extra-canonical sources placing pre-Constantine groups of Christians in Britain, who consider themselves to hold the original authority.

[27] Gonzalez details torture to death, drowning, and being drawn and quartered as well as discussing in detail the infamous inquisition killings.

years. I might add, among some of the best practicing Christians I have known have been devout Roman Catholics.

Among all of the Christian churches of which I am aware, the Holy Roman Catholic Church and the Church of Jesus Christ of Latter-day Saints are the only to claim priesthood authority directly from Jesus Christ. This is what the restoration of the Gospel of Jesus Christ is all about for a Mormon. I've attached a document from the church about this doctrine if you want to refresh your memory (Appendix D). Having authority to act in God's name within His church is also why it is so important that you are able to trace your priesthood lineage back to Jesus Christ.

CHAPTER II

OLD TESTAMENT ISSUES

Dear Dad,

I saw a NOVA program[28] the other night. Among other things it stated there is no archeological evidence to support the Adam and Eve story, Noah's flood, Abraham, and even the mass exodus of the Israelites from Egypt (suggesting Israelites were originally Canaanites). Skeptics say the Old Testament has no confirmation of the religiously related events. Is this true?

Dear Son,

Again, they are somewhat right and somewhat wrong. It is wrong to say there is, "no archeological evidence." One of the ways to validate the Old Testament is to find towns, cities, and names of people that are recorded there. Even evidence of battles and conquest are helpful in verifying the writings as authentic history. For instance, the Babylonian captivity and the fall of Jericho have been confirmed (although there is question about Joshua's participation in it). In addition the names of many locations, major political figures and some religious leaders seem to be, for the most part, unchallenged by the skeptics.

You may remember in Jeremiah 38:4 persecutions of prophets is mentioned. There has been an archeological discovery from Lachish, an outlaying town near Jerusalem. Some pieces of pottery (potsherds) with writings on them have been found. These are referred to as the Lachish Letters that indicated, among other things, governmental intentions to harm prophets who

---

[28] PBS airing on November 18, 2008, The Bible's Buried Secrets.

were judged to be undermining the morale of the city (under siege from Nebuchadnezzar).[29] In addition, an account is made on these potsherds that describe governmental representatives pursuing an unnamed prophet to Egypt and capturing him. This is very much like the account of Uriah in Jeremiah. Although Jeremiah is not specifically mentioned, some of the Lachish findings relate to specific incidents, including an unfamiliar prophet.

Another, archeological find[30] is a ninth century B.C. inscription on a stela (stone) called the Tel Dan Inscription. These writings include the phrases, "House of David" and "King of Israel." This is significant because so far it is the only archaeological evidence of a historical David whose existence has been hotly debated prior to this discovery. Skeptics have questioned the existence of the Temple of Solomon, in spite of strong religious traditions. Excavation attempts of the believed location of the Temple of Solomon have been inhibited because of tensions between Jews and Muslims. However, an excavation site near the believed temple site yielded a stone pomegranate that sits on top of a rod bearing the inscription, "Belonging to the Temple of Yahweh" (Yahweh being Jehovah). This leads some to conclude Solomon's Temple has been identified. The authenticity of the inscriptions is currently being investigated.[31]

---

[29] Nibley, Hugh W.

[30] *Bible History Daily* (BAS publication) www.biblicalarcheology.org. 07/17/2015.

[31] Biblical Archeology Review, a publication that focuses on archeological activity related to biblical issues provides a running commentary on challenges and discussions relating to the authenticity of this item. As of this writing, general opinion is that extreme caution should be used in considering the pomegranate inscription as authentic.

Some apologists enthusiastically claim cities of Sodom and Gomorra have been located. Clay tablets with writings were discovered in a destroyed ancient palace in Syria. Names are mentioned on these tablets that could be interpreted as Sodom and Gomorra.

In addition, there are some excavated cities with destruction that matches biblical events such as catastrophic burning and fallen structures. There are problems in both of these cases, for example, the dates do not match with biblical accounts or there is disagreement by scholars with the interpretations of the names of Sodom and Gomorrah found on the clay tablets. I've attached a document if you want to read more about this (see Appendix E).

One of the first biblical archeological explorations (1868 followed by 1907-1909) was inspired by Joshua chapter 11. This is the story of the Israelite conquest in the battle of Jericho, where the walls came tumbling down. Excavation disclosed the walls had tumbled down but were dated centuries before the Israelites entered the land. Here again, we have conflict from scholars. Hershel Shenks, editor of *Biblical Archeology Review* (BAR) concluded, "The conquest tradition in the Book of Joshua is therefore better seen as a literary, theological account, rather than an historical one."[32] Ammon Ben-Tor, writing an article for the *Biblical Archeology Review* concluded the dates allow for Israeli presence at the time of the fall of Jericho.[33] As with much

---

[32] Hershel Shenks in internet article 6/28/13.

[33] BAR 39:04 Jul/Aug 2013 by Ammon Ben-Tor. It should be noted, however, Israeli presence may well have accounted for the downfall of Jericho.

of ancient historical reconstruction, it is often difficult to be definitive about details one way or another.

There are also some Bedouin (nomadic desert dwelling tribal people) traditions that refer to Old Testament events. For example, there is a desert well that is now dried up but Bedouin tradition claims it as a well that Moses once used.[34]

Again, it appears there is meaningful confirmation of some sites and names correlating with Old Testament accounts, but confirmation of specific religious content is, for the most part, yet to be determined. For example, there is no concrete evidence to the parting of the Red Sea, nor independent data to support the migration of the Israelites once leaving Egypt, the location of Mt. Sinai, etc.

Always keep this in mind: missing information is not supportable proof that there is no information to be found; it merely leaves the question open. Again, the Old Testament, I believe, has established itself as a reasonably reliable chronicler of secular events, names, and locations. This is not a minor issue to a person with a spiritual testimony; the existing secular data is readily seen as confirmation. I'm sure you understand that to a skeptic, on the other hand, this same data would be assigned little importance due to the assumption that religious events are not real to begin with. Until all truth is revealed, only those willing to learn through the Sprit will feel confident in the teachings found In the Old Testament. Without the Spirit, we mortals are left with a reality in which any given person depends upon the information they attended to and the importance they ascribe to that information.

---

[34] National Geographic has a two page photograph and brief discussion of the well site.

CHAPTER III

NEW TESTAMENT ISSUES

Dear Dad,

Thanks, the research on the Old Testament looks like it can be pretty confusing when considering all points of view. I can see where people who do not have a spiritual testimony of the truthfulness of these things are coming from. I hope my own testimony can hold up to this. I've just run into a lot of issues about the New Testament.

Critics emphasize the unreliability of the New Testament. I'll list a few that have particularly bothered me:

1. Older versions of the New Testament vary when compared to newer versions. For Example Christian critic, Ben Yehoshua[35] says the first two chapters of Matthew, in earlier texts, did not include reference to the virgin birth but this was added later.

2. There seem to be contradictions within the scriptures themselves. For instance John 18:28 states the crucifixion was on Passover eve while Mark 15:1 & 25 says the crucifixion happened on the following day.[36] Another contradiction is after the resurrection, Luke 24:1-52 says the disciples stayed in Jerusalem until Jesus ascended to heaven. Matthew 28: 1-20,

---

[35] Ben Yehoshua (p. 14). I consider this author to be extremely biased but will cite him because his arguments represents others of similar inclinations.

[36] See Doherty (*Jesus Puzzle*, p. 43).

however, says the disciples went straight away to Galilee.[37]

3.   The scholars claim the names of apostles were assigned to the Gospel writings at a later time when in fact nobody knows who actually wrote them.

4.   Those who know the area John lived question the locations he mentions in his writings.

5.   There is the apparent fabrication (redaction) of some of Paul's letters by others. Using form analysis[38] as evidence, some scholars say many of Paul's letters (six of the thirteen) are a compilation of writings of various authors.[39]

When I read this stuff, I get pretty confused.

Son,

Your confusion is understandable. Interestingly, these are issues that caused a believing scholar I am familiar with to become a

---

[37] Ehrman (p. 170), states many such discrepancies, "... penetrate the Gospel traditions."

[38] Form analysis refers to various devised systems to examine written content in terms of types of words used and correspondence of content with other content to attempt to determine common and differing characteristics.

[39] Doherty (*Challenging*, p. 13), Frederich (p. 53), and Ehrman (p. 38) accept Romans, 1 and 2 Corinthians, Galatians, Philippians, I Thessalonians, and Philemon. The epistle to the Hebrews along with Timothy and Titus, Ephesians, and Colossians 1 and 2 are considered to be of an anonymous author.

prominent skeptic.[40] Hang in there; things get better as we consider the total picture. Remember, we are seeking truth and that is not always comfortable or immediate; it takes patience. I believe you will eventually reach the conclusions I have as long as you keep truth as the goal. Let us take the issues you mention one at a time. For clarity sake, I'll number my replies as you have numbered the questions.

1. With regard to Ben Yeshoua's writings, I have read his blog and consider him to be well informed but extremely biased against Christians. Yeshoua uses the Didache to argue against the virgin birth concept. The Didache is an accumulation of Jewish writings that include the story of Jesus birth, similar to that found in the Book of Matthew. This version evolved over time, originally not mentioning a virgin birth but later including it. As a result he argues that the Didache is the foundation for the Book of Matthew and the concept of a virgin birth was added over time. Others recognize a parallel in content with Matthew but do not agree that Matthew was derived from the Didache.[41] The early versions of Matthew have been widely studied and debated by scholars. One issue in the heart of the debate is the word "virgin" which can be translated either to mean "a young woman" or a "woman who has never had sexual intercourse". As a result, the translator can interject bias into the work.

---

[40] Jones (p. 23) mentions the discovery of discrepancies led to Bart Ehrman's serious questions regarding the reliability of the New Testament as a source of information and authorship of several books regarding the issues.

[41] Wikipedia, Didache.

2. Okay, to begin, there are some inconsistencies in the New Testament. You have listed some issues that have been discussed by scholars. In part, given the original oral traditions and variations that occur by copyists, perhaps some contradictions are to be expected. Some argue that variances confirm different authorship in the same way eyewitness accounts of the same event will vary. This would account for differences in the time or place that an event occurred. Apologists note, I think correctly, basic characteristics of the New Testament accounts remain intact. For example, some examples that are found in more than one of the Gospels are:

    A. Jesus existed as a human figure.
    B. Jesus performed miracles.
    C. Jesus taught of and prayed to His Father in Heaven.
    D. Jesus taught of an overriding principle of Love.
    E. Jesus appointed 12 Apostles.
    F. Jesus honored the practice of baptism.
    G. Jesus was resurrected.
    H. Jesus was of a divine nature.

3. It is true nobody knows who wrote the Gospels (Matthew, Mark, Luke & John). As we have already discussed we assume the scriptures were originally kept orally and written by different people over time in segments. According to scholars, the earliest written reference to portions of the New Testament is by Justin Martyr, *Memoirs of the Apostles,* around the middle of the second century.[42] To our knowledge, Irenaeus (a Christian about

---

[42] Doherty (*Challenging,* p. 8, 41).

AD 180) is the first to note the actual authors' names[43] of the Gospels. Peter and James are also judged by scholars to have been written by other unknown people.[44] Scholars speculate the apostles' names were used to give the scriptures apostolic authority. In my opinion, these scholars are probably correct. This should not, however, cause us to disregard the reliability of the scriptures. The reality is they represent events reported by people who were participants at the time and for the most part are consistent with each other.

4. Using the information we have at this time, it is true there are inconsistencies in the location of towns as named by John. Critics, to support the claim the accounts were merely generated in the second century, use contradictions such as these. On the other hand, one author, D. M. Smith, emphasizes John's accuracy in terms of describing in detail some aspects of the Jerusalem area such as the plan of the Temple and the Sheep Gate Pool of Bethesda, in addition to knowing Jesus is from Nazareth, not Bethlehem. It could be that John's inconsistencies are another item that can be added to the list of disparities generated by copyists, and translation differences we have previously discussed. In other cases the bible records Nazareth as being the hometown of Jesus. Interestingly, James F. Strange, an American archeologist, notes "Nazareth is not mentioned in ancient Jewish sources

---

[43] Doherty (*Challenging*, p. 9).

[44] Ehrman (p. 19 & 29), also notes Peter was banned by a bishop at the end of the second century but it was later adopted. With James the author is judged to be in the second half of the second century (p. 209).

earlier than the third century AD." [45] Obviously someone fabricating a religious story in AD 200 would not know to use the town Nazareth[46] as the hometown of Jesus. Of a similar nature Acts 14:6 places Iconium as a separate location from Lyconia. This was long considered by critics to be in error. Later, however, discoveries have confirmed the original Acts account.[47]

5. Remember the list of previously mentioned archeological finds we have already discussed? The tomb of Jesus, Peter's house, and the gravesite of Lazarus - all help add evidence for the validity of the New Testament. They were lost sites that were preserved by traditions of both the relatives of Jesus and others and were located at a later time.

6. With regard to the letters of Paul, scholars are able to pretty well document the majority of the letters (7 of the 13) using form analysis technique. The form analysis technique (vocabulary, writing style, modes of expression, frequencies of word patterns, and presupposed historical situation) is not an exact science and there is much to be done before one can have total confidence in the conclusions of the analyses. Are there writings attributed

---

[45] Wikipedia, Nazareth

[46] Probably best said at this point in time, Nazareth was not popularly recognized until AD 300 and is currently contested as being populated at the time of Jesus. At the same time, it is contended by archaeologist Yardenna Alexandre to be confirmed as a place of residence during Jesus' time.

[47] McDowell (p. 64), a well-published apologist, notes Cicero, (106-43 BC) was one who leveled the original criticism.

to Paul in fact written by someone else? I'm not sure and we may never be sure, however, keep in mind the consistency of the spiritual teachings found in the texts. Ask yourself, "are the teachings helpful in the spiritual sense or not?" Perhaps this is not a question to stump the skeptic, but it is a legitimate inquiry for the seeker of truth.

I think there are two important, points of logic defending the validity of the accounts in the New Testament. The first is the inclusion of information that is contrary to social wisdom of the time (in some discourses referred to as "zeitgeist"[48]). The report by females that Jesus had arisen is a good example. In that day, females were not accepted as legitimate witnesses therefore, the account supports legitimacy by going against what would have been socially acceptable. The second point is that the death of Jesus should have ended the movement, as was the case with other leaders and rumored messiahs of the time. Instead, the Christian movement gained strength and flourished in spite of very severe persecution. This suggests the early Christians were strongly motivated by something extraordinary. The resurrection of Jesus could account for this motivation.

Now, these points are significant to me because as a believer because it is a compatible explanation from my viewpoint but do not carry the exceptional weight required by skeptics, who are looking for exceptional empirical evidence. Still they are legitimate points of support.

---

[48] The thinking of the times (zeitgeist) is a strong force focusing the thinking of people. To go against this flow signals some significant force, outside of the culture, influencing it. See Appendix H.

Dad,

I liked your question about "are the teachings helpful in a spiritual sense." You're right, that's not something to help the skeptics, but it helps me in my search for truth. I've appreciated your help regarding inconsistencies in the text. The parallels to the life of Jesus and pagan myths confuse me. For example Adonis, Dionysus, Osiris, and Zoroaster were claimed to be products of divinely impregnated virgin births.[49] There also seems to be parallels in pagan myths to names that are the same as the apostles' names. Obviously this makes it look like the stories of Jesus came from pagan myths. This is all being presented as sources for biblical accounts.

Dear Son,

I am glad to have been helpful. You bring up the mythological approach, which appears rather frequently, and when viewed in isolation, seems pretty compelling.
I want to tell you of a huge "ah ha!" moment for your mom on this same issue. While at a biological cell differentiation seminar, your mom met an author of a well-known biology textbook. This man was quite verbal in his disdain for the use of a few of his statements to support creationism that, as you know, is a rejection of secular evolution. Later, when this author gave his PowerPoint presentation to the group he mocked religious thought by using the myths you are mentioning to create an evolutionary tree to several Biblical accounts. As your mom sat, feeling as uncomfortable as you probably feel now, the idea came to her; with evolution, there is common origin. For her, this clarified everything. The creation story was given anciently, as

---

[49] Ben Yeshousha (p. 14). Archarya bases most of her book on the accounts of Jesus citing many examples from mythology.

were most of the details of Christ's birth and life. To her it became clear that the common origins were the truth. And truth became corrupted (or evolved) over the years to become pagan myths and indigenous stories.

In addition to your mom's experience and insight, there is another fallacy in drawing parallels between myths and religious events. I would refer to it as "cherry-picking" information. Let me provide an example of the potential misuse by comparing President Lincoln and President Kennedy. This information comes from an undocumented paper sold in the gift shop at Ford's Theater in Washington, D.C. With it, I will point out characteristics that could be interpreted as implying some (mystical?) connection between the two:

- Lincoln was elected president in 1860, Kennedy in 1960.
- The names Lincoln and Kennedy each contain seven letters.
- Both Lincoln and Kennedy were concerned with Civil Rights.
- Both Presidents' wives lost children through death while in the White House.
- Men whose names start with "G" opposed both Lincoln and Kennedy for re-election.
- Both were slain on a Friday and in the presence of their wives.
- Lincoln's secretary, whose name was Kennedy, advised him not to go to the theatre. While, Kennedy's secretary, whose name was Lincoln, advised him not to go to Dallas.
- Both of their successors were southern Democrats named Johnson, and were in the Senate.
- Andrew Johnson was born in 1808 and Lyndon Johnson was born in 1908.

- The names Andrew Johnson and Lyndon Johnson each contain thirteen letters.
- John Wilkes Booth (who assassinated Lincoln) was born in 1839 and Lee Harvey Oswald (who assassinated Kennedy) was born in 1939.
- Both Oswald and Booth were southerners favoring unpopular ideas.
- John Wilkes Booth shot Lincoln in a theatre and ran to a warehouse.
- Lee Harvey Oswald shot Kennedy from a warehouse and ran to a theatre.
- The names John Wilkes Booth and lee Harvey Oswald each contain fifteen letters.
- Both assassins were killed before being brought to trial.

From these common elements, we could conclude there is a relationship operating that is common to the two. A thousand years from now, a person given this document could easily conclude Kennedy, the later character, was merely a fabrication of the Lincoln story. This is because the innumerable differences between the two have been ignored and information was "cherry-picked" favoring only the common elements. Again, truth for any given person is the information they pay attention to and the importance given to it. It is important to pay attention to what is not said as well as what is said.

As can be seen by this example, there is a flaw in the "cherry-picking" method. When presented with a variety of data those aspects that agree with a predetermined conclusion are chosen and then presented as proof of the final event. This is in direct conflict with the very scientific process that is presented as the keystone of many of the challenges to religious belief.

Thanks Dad,

I'd never heard mom's story before and I found your example of Lincoln and Kennedy interesting. I guess I'll have to think about this. It seems like there is cherry-picking on both sides.

What do you know about a guy named Apollonius? Some say the story of Jesus came from Apollonius.

Son,

Apollonius was a philosopher who existed in a similar time frame to Jesus. In an effort to impede the rising tide of Christianity, the wife of a Roman emperor in 217 A.D. commissioned Philostratus, to write an account of Apollonius' life. [50]Philostratus claimed he derived his accounts from a follower of Apollonius. Most scholars agree that Philostratus was a careless historian and probably embellished the accounts including similar miracles to Jesus. The question here again is, what came first? In my opinion the purpose of writing an account of Apollonius' life was to put into question the validity of Jesus. Because the accounts of Jesus could be used as a source, it is entirely possible that the stories of Apollonius are actually taken from the stories of Jesus. Other than the account of Philostratus, the earlier accounts for Apollonius do not show much of a parallel.[51]

---

[50] Magee (p.3)

[51] Internet discussion by Magee. See also discussion of what is actually documented in Wikipedia, *Apollonius of Tyana*.

Dad,

All right. How about the Talmud? How strong are the critics claims concerning the parallels found in the Talmud and the stories of Jesus? [52]

Son,

    I do know about these stories and the controversies around them. Many scholars seriously challenge the reliability of the Talmud. Remember the Talmud is a series of stories, and the ones you are referring to were written for the most part in the third century and later.[53] They reference people, some of whom, performed similar acts as Jesus. However, Jesus is never mentioned by name. Some apologists, Klausner in particular, consider these stories to actually be an indirect reference (or disguised references) for Jesus of Nazareth.[54] There are also accounts in various other writings (including the New Testament) that refer to individuals alleged to have performed miracles. My opinion is that some of the individuals discussed, may have some basis in reality, but are not related to Jesus and therefore are not relevant.[55]

---

[52] The *Talmud* contains the teachings and opinions of thousands of rabbis on a variety of subjects, including *Halakha* (law), Jewish ethics, philosophy, customs, history, lore and many other topics. The *Talmud* is the basis for all codes of Jewish law and is much quoted in rabbinic literature.

[53] Doherty (*Challenging*, p. 232-23) states all Jewish references in the Talmud come from the third century and later and are usually wildly inconsistent with the Gospels even to the extent of locating Jesus in the wrong century.

[54] Klausner (p. 46), lists 11 parallel similar events but the time frames are not harmonious with the New Testament accounts of Jesus.

[55] Doherty (p.84cv) & Gjorgievski (p.4) provide good summaries.

Dear Dad,

Thanks for your quick response. Let me give you another one. Critics consider Old Testament quotes that are believed by Christians to predict Jesus of Nazareth as the Messiah to be, "… a fantasy of misreading the ancient passages, ignoring the contexts they are found in, glossing over the vast variety and contradictions within these alleged prophecies …"[56] As an example, I just read a critic's argument where he attacks the New Testament account of Jesus' last days. This includes the trial, crucifixion and resurrection as being a reworking of the "age-old genre of Jewish writing about the Suffering and Vindication of the Innocent Righteous One."[57] Skeptics contend the "Jesus Story" was made up to fit the prophecies. Isn't this an example of cherry-picking?

Dear Son,

As you know, Latter-day Saints recognize Jesus Christ as the God of the Old Testament and therefore relate the entire text to Him. Without that perspective, I can understand how Old Testament prophecies can more easily be cited as an example of "cherry-picking." To counter this argument, the apologist McDowell states there are at least 300 Old Testament prophecies of which he lists 60 specific parallels between the prophecies of the Messiah and fulfillment in the New Testament.[58] To illustrate, I will list two here.

---

[56] Doherty (Challenging, p. 232-33).

[57] Ibid

[58] McDowell (p. 164-192).

- Isaiah 7:14: "Therefore the Lord Himself will give you a sign: Behold, the virgin shall conceive and bear a Son and shall call His name Immanuel." (Fulfilled in Matthew 1:18, 24, 25, & Luke 1: 26-35).
- Psalm 2:7, I Chr. 17:11-14 & 2 Sam. 7:12-16, "I will declare the decree: The Lord has said to me, 'you are my Son, today I have begotten you'. And suddenly a voice came from heaven, saying, 'This is My beloved Son, in whom I am well pleased." (Fulfilled in Matthew 3:17 & 16:16, Mark 9:7, Luke 9:35 & 22:70, Acts 31:30-33, and John 1:34 & 49).

In my opinion, the citations referred to provide a quantity and specificity of match to strongly tip the scales in favor of Jesus being the predicted Messiah. This again, however, is my interpretation of the data and, as earlier mentioned, others interpret it otherwise. Once you have considered these parallels, McDowell[59] notes these prophecies were beyond the control of anyone to engineer such events and/or they were beyond chance happenings.

The following sources provide good evidence to support the scriptures.

- The cultural importance of accurately memorizing scripture.
- The supporting documents from varying areas of the world.
- The supporting archaeological evidence.
- The statements by the Greek and Roman writers.

Throughout our discussion of the canonized scriptures (Old and New Testaments), in my opinion we have reasonable empirical evidence to support the validity of scripture. I doubt, however, we have sufficient empirical support to be meaningful

---

[59] McDowell (p. 193).

to a skeptic. For those who do not readily accept ideas of divine intervention in men's lives and miracles, a much stronger case needs to be made. Again, "extraordinary claims require extraordinary evidence."[60]

Dear Dad,

As the objections are looked at, I have a question. What evidence would be meaningful to a skeptic? Is there anything that is acceptable to them?

Son,

Regarding a skeptical position, the truth is unless a skeptic is willing to look at religion with the same open mind they expect from you, not much will convince them. One reason I have spent so much time on this stuff is not to convince the critic but to point out to you that their arguments are often biased and not all they claim they are. I know you are being bombarded with "scholarly" argument that is designed to shake your faith. These positions project so much authority that I think it's important for you to see how flawed they can be.

In honest scientific thinking, without defensive emotion, no conclusion is absolutely fixed, no possibility absolutely excluded. It cannot legitimately be concluded that religion is invalid or that there is no God (proving nonexistence is not possible in any sense). At the same time, just because there is, scientifically, always an open question, it does not prove the existence of a God or the absolute validity of religion.

---

[60] Carl Sagan is most often quoted with this phrase although other philosophers have posed it. See Wikipedia for a discussion, including the requirement of probability theory (Bayesian) in providing evidence.

In my opinion, at this point, the most practical approach would be to provide data that could not be reasonably explained other than by the religious alternative. I like to think of it as an approach similar to a court of law. In most courts of law, the preponderance of evidence establishes a fact; is it more likely than not? Facts of the validity of the claim must be established "beyond a reasonable doubt," not "beyond the shadow of a doubt" as some T.V. lawyers like to say.[61]

Up to this point, many believers of Christianity would be satisfied with the data as sufficient to support the religious claims. To a skeptic, who defines such things as resurrection from the dead,[62] walking on water, parting of the sea, and divine intervention in healing as extraordinary, a very high standard is required. Let's look at the rest of the data and then judge.

---

[61] Paraphrased comments of Charlie Burnett, attorney and personal friend.

[62] Interestingly, resurrection may not be as far removed from accepted thinking as one might think. For example, there are many examples of "near death experiences" where all clinical signs of life are absent but then later return. If one considers, however, the brutal scourging Jesus received along with the crucifixion process, an exceptional case presents itself. Tipler, a physicist, extrapolates from quantum mechanics to explain the feasibility of resurrection requiring exceptionally large amounts of energy. One other interesting issue is a "Shroud of Turin". There is in Turin, France, a shroud that is believed to have been used to cover the body of Christ after the crucifixion and bears an image of Him. See Appendix F for a brief discussion.

CHAPTER IV

BOOK OF MORMON ISSUES

Dear Dad,

Without faith as I see it, there is not a slam-dunk on either side of the fence. One could go either way with the evidence.

Dear Son,

I agree with your assessment. Faith of course is the fundamental principle regarding our spiritual growth. Still, that isn't what you are dealing with is it? There is enough evidence supporting the scriptures and the existence of Jesus Christ for one who desires to accept that but for the person choosing to believe otherwise, there is reasonable room for that too.

However, there is a little more, hang in there with me on this.

We haven't talked about the Book of Mormon yet. Remember, it is another testament of Jesus Christ. The purpose of the Book of Mormon is to remind us of the covenants that were made for our benefit and to convince the Jew and the Gentile that Jesus is the Christ. With this in mind, let's take an objective look at the Book of Mormon. I know you were raised with the information of how the Book of Mormon came to be. I have attached, a quick synopsis (Appendix J) in case you want a reminder.

For me, the Book of Mormon has been where I have found a solid ground when evidences and arguments surrounding the Bible cause me to question.

Dad,

Ok Dad, speaking of the Book of Mormon, I was surfing the net and came across a book called, A *View of the Hebrews* and a book I have heard about before called the *Spaulding Manuscript*. Some say the *Book of* Mormon is nothing more than a copying of portions of these two books; "a mere reflection of elements of thought that were common to the existing culture and not of divine origin." This sounds to me like the same attacks that we get about the Old and New Testaments, claiming they came from the cultural influences, something other than God.

Dear Son,

I know what you are talking about. I've seen some videos and YouTube presentations that can be pretty convincing. As a matter of fact I just sat through a rather lengthy Internet blog by a group attempting to discourage people from affiliating with the Latter-day Saint Church. In a low-key, friendly, fatherly, almost condescending tone, the presenter stated there were signed affidavits from people certifying that many names found in the Book of Mormon originated in a document called the *Spaulding Manuscript*. His sincere tone was incredibly disingenuous when we take time to examine the facts. When you consider any one presentation alone, it can be pretty convincing. Sometimes, what is not said is more important than what is said. As with the critical presentation of the Old and New Testaments, the broader picture needs to be looked at, both confirming data and contradictory data.

Reverend Spaulding wrote a story (around 1812[63]) about a Roman ship having blown off course thereby discovering the Americas. He wrote this story while living in Ohio and occasionally

---

[63] Wikipedia, Spaulding Manuscript

he read this story to his neighbors and tried to publish in Pittsburgh, PA. Critics claimed this story paralleled and included many of the proper names found in the Book of Mormon. Following publication of the Book of Mormon in 1830, critics produced written affidavits from alleged witnesses supporting their claim. When these charges were made however, Reverend Spaulding was dead and no one could produce a copy of his story to compare with the Book of Mormon. A few years later, a copy of the manuscript was found in a trunk of Rev. Spaulding's belongings. It bore almost no resemblance to the Book of Mormon story and did not include proper names that matched any found in the Book of Mormon.[64] The newly formed Church, The Church of Jesus Christ of Latter-day Saints, actually published a copy of the *Spaulding Manuscript* to dispel this argument because it clearly did not represent the Book of Mormon. The original copy of the Spaulding manuscript currently resides in the library of Oberlin College in Ohio. You can get a copy of the manuscript if you are interested.

The claims regarding *View of the Hebrews* by Ethan Smith (no relation to Joseph Smith), in my opinion, are a little more credible. This book was published about 5 years prior to the Book of Mormon. In his book, Ethan Smith asserted the North American Indians are descendants of the 10 Lost Tribes of Israel[65] who came over the Bering Straits. A book by David Persuitte strongly

---

[64] Anderson, discusses several issues related to the lack of relationship between the two manuscripts.

[65] Porter & Meldrum also provide contemporary evidence supporting this position; at least in terms of Hebrew evidence among North American tribes.

supports the *View of the Hebrews* and *Spaulding Manuscript* as being sources of the Book of Mormon.[66]

Like the *Spaulding Manuscript*, it is highly doubtful that Joseph Smith ever had access to or knew about the *View of the Hebrews*[67] before or during the translation of the Book of Mormon.

In an honest search for truth, several Latter-day Saint historians have examined the recognized parallel themes between the Book of Mormon and the *View of the Hebrews*. Neither the overall story line nor the spiritual teachings of the Book of Mormon can be likened to the *View of the Hebrews*. As an example, I have included an attachment of the work of Charles Gee, a Church historian as Appendix G. The *View of Hebrews* can also be found through online or at a bookstore if you want to make your own comparisons

Having read it myself, I find it difficult to understand how anyone who is familiar with the Book of Mormon would consider the *View of the Hebrews* as being a source book. In my opinion, *View of the Hebrews* represents thinking of the times and the

---

[66] A critical review of Persuitte's book is provided by www.mormonthink.com/mormonstudiesreview2.htm and www.FairMormon.org.

[67] It is believed a university, near to the location of Joseph Smith, had a copy of *View of the Hebrews* in its library. Joseph Smith was never characterized as reading anything other than the *Bible* (and his mother stated he had not even read all of that). At the time of the writing of the *Book of Mormon*, Joseph Smith was described by critics as (inaccurately) ignorant and (accurately) uneducated and is highly unlikely to have read the *View of the Hebrews* before or during translating the *Book of Mormon*. There is no direct evidence he or his associates had any knowledge of it although there is a possibility some of them are likely to have some at least indirect contact or knowledge of it. Years later, Joseph Smith did cite *View of the Hebrews* as evidence of a link between the Jews and the American Indians in an attempt to give some credibility to the *Book of Mormon* at the time.

Book of Mormon, while having some similarities, is often contrary to that flow, contrary to the zeitgeist. For instance, in his book, as I mentioned, Ethan Smith drives home the message the 10 Lost Tribes came over the Bering Straits and were among the forerunners to the American Natives.[68] The Bering Strait migration theory was first proposed in the 1500's and is still widely accepted today. For anyone of the time concocting a story they would want to be taken seriously, the Bering Strait theory or a similar Northern migration would be used. The Book of Mormon does not challenge the Bering Strait nor a Northern migration; it merely ignores it altogether and, very importantly, describes a route that went against the grain of thinking at the time it was written.[69] This is a critical issue and should not be ignored.

Dear Dad,

I ran across a book written by Church members where they compare Joseph Smith's thinking and writing style to the Book of Mormon and suggest he made it up.

---

[68] Charles C. Mann, (Kindle location 2946) points out the strong opinion of the times was stated by Acosta in 1590 ,"... we would have to say that they **crossed not by sailing on the sea, but by walking on land**. And they followed this way quite unthinkingly, changing places and lands little by little, with some of them settling in the lands already discovered and others seeking new ones." [Emphasis added by Mann]. Mann emphasizes how this view continued into later times, particularly being championed by experts of the Smithsonian Institute to the extent of ridiculing and ignoring alternative hypotheses.

[69] Mann specifically mentions (Kindle location 2950) the *Book of Mormon* as varying from the opinions of people such as William Penn and, "... the famed minister Cotton Mather" In addition, Mann notes a dozen groups other than Jewish origin being hypothesized by others. including, ". . . Chinese, Romans, Africans, 'Hindoos', ancient Egyptians". This is important because it highlights the origin of the *Book of Mormon* concepts coming from sources other than the popular thinking (zeitgeist) of the times.

Also, what about the weird names in the Book of Mormon?

Son,

I want to remind you of the strong emotion aroused by religious subjects. This is true by some Church members who have a desire to present themselves as intellectually above supernatural thinking. If you are interested, I have attached some brief related comments (Appendix B).

I think it's somewhat presumptuous for experts of today to conclude that Joseph Smith's writing ability could match the level of complexity found in the Book of Mormon. They seem to ignore the following, often quoted, statement from Emma Smith, wife of Joseph, who knew him better than anyone. She had daily experience with Joseph Smith, scribed during some of the translation, and handled the metal plates.

I wrote for Joseph Smith during the work of translation. ...The larger part of this labor was done (in) my presence and where I could see and know what was being done. ... During no part of it did Joseph Smith have any mss. (manuscripts) or book of any kind from which to read or dictate except the metallic (sic) plates which I knew he had. Joseph Smith could neither write nor dictate a coherent and well-worded letter, let alone dictate a book like the Book of Mormon. ... (F)or one so ignorant (uneducated?) and unlearned as he was, it was simply impossible.[70]

---

[70] Daniel C. Peterson in Reynolds, (p. 160). See p. 173 footnote 55 for a more detailed reference to this particular quote.

However, presumptuous or not, let's take a look at some of the analyses that have been done. The analysis of Joseph Smith's writing compared to the writing of the Book of Mormon has been used both for and against it being given by revelation (remember cherry-picking ?). I consider the conclusions drawn from style analysis to be easily influenced through bias and I recommend we use judgment when considering.

To directly answer your question, I have some examples.

We have previously discussed the similarities claimed between contemporary sources like the *Spaulding Manuscript*. Some writing analysts note a flavor of Joseph Smith's style of writing in the Book of Mormon phrasing. I have to admit; I don't know the process for translation through revelation. Did the Spirit dictate it given word for word or were impressions given and then formatted by Joseph Smith or his scribes? If the latter is true, we would expect to see some remnants of his style in the writing.

On the other hand, to support authenticity, this writing analysis method has been used to demonstrate similarities in ancient Jewish writings with the Book of Mormon. For example, there are Hebrew phrases found throughout the Book of Mormon as well as the presence of Chiasmus, a pattern of inverted repetition in ancient Hebrew writings not likely to have been familiar to or deliberately replicated by Joseph Smith or his associates.[71]

---

[71] Welch notes, Chiasmus was first noticed by a few nineteenth century pioneer theologians in Germany and England, but the idea had to wait until the 1930's before it found an ardent exponent, Nils Lund, who was able to lay the principle before the eyes of the world in a convincing way. But even at that it was not until the decade of the 1960's, after much more had been learned about the philology of early Semitic languages that chiasmus was properly understood and unequivocally acknowledged.

There have been questions raised on the proper names found in the Book of Mormon. One name in particular, Alma, was held up as a point of derision because while Alma, a prominent male name in the Book of Mormon, was clearly and without question a female name in Joseph Smith's culture. Even today we find writers criticizing the use of the name Alma for a male character.[72]

Because of his lack of formal education, some concluded this name was chosen out of ignorance, either being taken from the phrase "Alma Mater" or from the name of a town in New York. The town argument is moot as the town of Alma was established in 1856 over 20 years after the publishing of the Book of Mormon. I think this is another example of going against the zeitgeist (trend of popular thinking of the time). Joseph Smith did not just make this up. He received this name exactly as he claimed, through revelation. This is supported by a 20th century discovery. Some first-hand writings were unearthed in the Dead Sea area, dated around AD 130. One letter referenced a man leaving property to his son, Alma.[73] And so we see that Alma is an ancient Hebrew male name, a fact that Joseph Smith was obviously not privy to. In my personal search of known information, I have found criticisms to actually lead to validation

---

[72] McDowell (p. 288-89).

[73] Parry & Ricks note in the early 1960's an Israeli archaeologist excavated a cave located west of the Dead Sea where a number of artifacts were discovered. Among them was a bundle of papyrus documents that included deeds belonging to the leader of the Second Jewish Revolt (AD 132-35), Shimeon bar Kosiba. Among the documents was a land-lease agreement written in Hebrew mentioning Alma, the son of Judah. The male name of Alma was apparently familiar to ancient men of the area (p. 79-82).

of Joseph Smith's accounts. (See Appendix I for more discussion on this).

It has always been common practice for parents to name their children using cultural roots. This is another area that is studied to demonstrate cultural influences regarding the authenticity of the Book of Mormon. Again personal bias can be a determining factor. For instance, I came across a critic on the web who contended many of the Book of Mormon names had common roots, therefore they were fabricated.[74] On the other hand, scholars find analysis of the common roots to be characteristic of ancient Jewish writings thus supporting the Book of Mormon account.[75] If you want to see more about what I am talking about, I have attached an example as Appendix J.

---

[74] Ashment (p.375) engaged in examining percentages of occurrences of English Apodosis, in the King James edition of the Old Testament, an ancient Jeremiah, and the Book of Mormon demonstrating a relationship of the King James wording and the Book of Mormon wording. Interestingly, and not noted by Ashment, was that two of his four results demonstrated a closer resemblance of the Book of Mormon and the ancient Jeremiah relationship than the King James and ancient Jeremiah. Sometimes investigators represent a means of approach that involves considerable cognitive gymnastics and, while it is intellectually engaging and interesting, a person can become so focused on this thinking that the broader picture is ignored.

[75] John L. Hilton employed analysis of variance (my characterization) statistical procedures along with "conservative" (rigid) selection categories to demonstrate differences in writing style between two major *Book of Mormon* authors as distinct from the writing styles or the three most likely contemporary authors, "...it is statistically indefensible to propose Joseph Smith or Oliver Cowdery or Solomon Spaulding as the author of the 30,000 words from the Book of Mormon manuscript attributed to Nephi & Alma." (p. 225-258).

Dad,

What about archeological evidence? I find several critics saying there is no archeological evidence supporting the Book of Mormon.[76] Some point out there are things mentioned in the Book of Mormon that did not exist in the New World until after Columbus. Examples are silk, sheep, asses, horses, and elephants (mentioned in Ether 9).[77] Metal weapons, iron, steel, brass, plows, chariots, and chains are also cited as mentioned in *the* Book of Mormon but were things not known in early Mesoamerica.

Dear Son,

I guess my immediate response is to paraphrase Mark Twain, "The lack of archeological (empirical) evidence for the Book of Mormon is greatly exaggerated." This reminds me of the same criticism being leveled at the Old and New Testaments, even today, to which a Christian apologist replied,[78] "... we have more and better historical documentation for Jesus than for any other religious founder (e.g. Zoroaster, Buddha, or Mohammed)."

Speaking of historical documentation, there is, in fact, specific archeological evidence of the Book of Mormon. While archaeological exploration has not been as extensive as Middle

---

[76] Muncaster (p.16) stated archeologists who searched the Americas found no evidence relating to the Book of Mormon. Doherty (p.77cv) noted that, relative to the data contained in the *Book of Mormon*, "... archeology has yet to confirm the existence of any person or place in that book, to uncover any artifacts, or any inscriptions relating to the Mormon myth." Likewise Acharya (p.107) noted, "Archeology has proven to be devastating for the Book of Mormon. Archeologists repeatedly failed to substantiate its claims..."

[77] Wikipedia, Archeology and the Book of Mormon.

[78] Mc Dowell (p.136) citing Edwin Yamauchi, a professor of history.

Eastern exploration, the Mesoamerican exploration is healthy and just coming of age.

A major part of the problem with excavating Book of Mormon archaeological evidence has been uncertainty where the events actually took place. Latter-day Saint author, Allan Norman, however, claims a review of all data has allowed him to pose a more accurate map that encompasses Mesoamerica, including part of Mexico. It should be mentioned also that other authors[79] present arguments for a North American location.

I personally have been impressed with research in the area and will include some of the findings. Until recently, Mesoamerican exploration was primarily limited to the Incan, Aztec, and Mayan groups that date later than most of the Book of Mormon accounts. Recently, archeological investigation of the pre- Columbian (Olmec) societies, now widely identified as the first major civilization in Mexico and predating the others (3,000 BC) are more likely related to most of the Book of Mormon incidents.[80]

To the best of my knowledge, at this time, there are several specific things mentioned in the Book of Mormon that have not yet been confirmed such as chariots, sheep, chains, and wheat. The most critics can say about this is that they have not yet been discovered. I will list some, but not all, evidence that

---

[79] Porter and Meldrum cite sources within Latter-day Saint literature, including wording in the *Book of Mormon* to argue a North American location for the *Book of Mormon* events. For the purposes of this discussion, I am focusing on verifiable empirical evidence, regardless of the source. (See Appendix G)

[80] Charles Mann, a non LDS author, provides a very comprehensive and objectively written account of pre-Columbian South American and Mexican cultures.

supports the Book of Mormon that, in the past, had been claimed by critics to be totally lacking in archeological evidence.

I am really impressed with an eight hundred-page book by J. Allen and B. Allen called *Exploring the Lands of the* Book of Mormon as well as several other sources you will see cited throughout the following list. The data they cite regarding ancient Olmec documents,[81] and their use of current maps to identify locations, bring to light similarities of societal structures, events and geographical details supported by archeological finds. Their findings are so abundant and detailed that it would be unreasonable to make a cherry-picking argument.[82] For simplicity sake I will bullet some of their findings.

- Ancient writings on the temple of the cross at Palenque: The Temple of the Cross is the largest and most significant pyramid within a complex of temples at the Maya ruins of Palenque in the state of Chiapas in Mexico.[83] They bear the genealogy and ascension to the throne of King Kish in 967 BC. This correlates nicely with the figure Kish found in the Book of Ether (10:17 & 18). Ether also describes the building of a great city following Kish's reign that is consistent with archaeological findings of massive building

---

[81] Allen & Allen (p. 131).

[82] There is considerable controversy around presence or absence of DNA evidence. The sum and substance is, at this time, experts in DNA consider it to be confused enough that the Book of Mormon can neither be proved nor disproved using it. See Appendix G for further discussion.

[83] Wikipedia *Temple of the Cross Complex*

programs of the same time period.[84]

- The method of city fortification found in the Book of Mormon matches those found in various locations throughout Mesoamerica.[85] For example, Alma 49-50 describes fortification of a city with a, "highness of the bank which had been thrown up, and the depth of the ditch which had been dug round about." A defensive earthworks surrounding the pre-classic period city of Becan as having a fortified earthworks and trenches[86] matches the Book of Mormon description in great detail. It is also a location that fits the hypothesized Mesoamerican city of Bountiful of the Book of Mormon. There are several similar examples that have been discovered as well.

- The *Book of Ether* (9:2), in the Book of Mormon mentions elephants, as you have mentioned; a claim ridiculed by critics. Archeological findings of skulls and primitive art provide evidence to the contrary. One author commented, "There can no longer be any doubt that man and elephant coexisted in America. This author presents evidence that men and domesticated elephants existed in the Americas,

---

[84] Allen & Allen (p. 501).

[85] Norman (p. 3).

[86] Allen & Allen (p. 94).brief summary statement. (p. 598-602) Detail a point by point comparison of an archeological description with Alma 49-50.

"as recently as 3,000 years ago."[87] While this article appeared in 1952, there are still today critics continuing to use this as an argument to disclaim the validity of the Book of Mormon.

- It is a common belief horses came to Mesoamerica at the time of the Spanish conquest. There are, however, pictures of horses and asses found in ancient Mexican hieroglyphs.[88] The Maya Room of the National Museum of Anthropology in Mexico City occasionally displays horse bones dated to the Book of Mormon times.[89]

- As you noted, earlier, chariots (and more specifically have wheels) were also mentioned as exceptions. However, there are Olmec era toy animals having wheels fashioned from stone.[90] While wheels on chariots have not yet been found, the Olmecs understood and used the principle of the wheel.

- You asked about criticism of various kinds of metals such as brass and iron mentioned in the Book of Mormon but

---

[87] Ludwell H. Johnson (p. 220-221). Also, Christofer Nobel Urlaub presents, on his website, photographs and accounts supporting his contention. There are also other, detailed documentation of a similar nature on the internet.

[88] Acharya (p. 400).

[89] Allen & Allen (p. 362).

[90] Mann, (Kindle location 4561-4571).

not found by archeologists. The following quote is taken from www.fairmormon.org:[91]

> "Brass" is an alloy of copper and zinc. It is a term used frequently in the Bible and the Book of Mormon. Biblical scholars suggest that rather than actual brass, scriptural references could have really been referring to bronze (an alloy of copper and tin). On the other hand, actual brass has been found in the Old World that dates to Lehi's era (500 BC), and so the idea of 'brass' plates once thought ridiculous is instead very credible. Either 'brass plates' or 'bronze plates' would fit. An interesting point concerning alloys is found in Ether 10:23 in which the Jaredites 'did make...brass,' (an alloy), but 'did dig...to get ore of gold, and of silver, and of iron, and of copper." The Book of Mormon author has a clear understanding of those metals that are found in a raw state, and those which must be made as an alloy.[92]

- The criticism regarding Iron is also in error as the discovery of Iron is documented as early as 1200 BC in Mesoamerica.[93]

---

[91] I recommend www.bookofmormoncentral.org, fairmormon.org and jefflindsay.com as three internet sources that are balanced and factual sources for any person of good will looking for usable data.

[92] Sorenson.

[93] Mann, (Kindle Location 4329). Mann mentions the fall of an Olmec society, San Loenzo as having iron beads (and rubber ax-head straps). Also see Allen & Allen p. 365. See also Allen & Allen p.365 notes pre-Columbian metal weapons

- You mentioned the conflict of silk being mentioned in the Book of Mormon. Apparently there are no silkworms in Mesoamerica, however, there has been discovered woven material that has the characteristics of silk.[94] Pearl S. Buck, in her book *Imperial Woman* refers to "silk" garments in ancient China that were made from pineapple fiber (readily obtainable in Mesoamerica). It is reasonable to say ancient terms for silk did not refer merely to the product produced by silkworms, even in China.

- If you haven't yet, you will probably come across some alleged discrepancies from the Book of Mormon witness' accounts regarding what the plates looked like. A note of interest, I think, is a discussion on the rings that bound the Book of Mormon plates together. David Whitmer, one of the witnesses who saw the Book of Mormon plates, during an 1877 interview, drew the shape of the rings as D shaped. The curator of the Early Office Museum in London, notes D shaped ring binders were not developed until the 1940's or 1950's. This method of binding plates was not in the culture at David Whitmer's time.[95] Around the mid-20th century, "an undisputed set of ancient gold plates were unearthed in a field consisting of six small gold sheets, finely inscribed and were bound by two D-shaped rings." This finding was dated about 600 B.C., the same

---

and other metal objects, including iron dating to 800 B.C. in the Olmec museum of Santiago, Tuxtla. See also Mann, (Kindle location 176).

[94] Gutfield & Haber.

[95] Aston, Warren. Meridian Magazine

period as the beginning of the Book of Mormon account. There is considerably more evidence and it's continually emerging. A quick Internet search under Book of Mormon, Gold Plates will give you what is current.[96]

- Com was the name of two kings from the Book of Mormon (*Ether* 1:4, 9:2, 10:5, 11:3) one dating about 600 B.C. and the other much earlier. This is interesting because a sixteenth-century Catholic Bishop named Landa compiled the cultural and oral traditions of the Yucatan. Briefly, the account specifies the lineage of the people as having come from "the place of the Com tribe." [97]

- Another charge by critics has been the fact that there is no written language among the 400 A.D. Incas. They conclude that the Book of Mormon is therefore in error as it is a written document. In 2006 A.D. an inscribed stone slab from the Olmec period was discovered in Veracruz, demonstrating a written language that parallels by time, and perhaps place, of the Book of Mormon events.[98]

- R. Meldrum, a Latter-day Saint author discusses several stones discovered in the North American Hopewell

[96] As a point of interest, while now the use of metal plates for record keeping in ancient times is well documented, the gold plates of King Darius incorporate several issues common to the plates Joseph Smith found. They were documents on gold plates, encased in a stone box.

[97] Allen & Allen (p. 299)

[98] Allen & Allen (p. 500-02)

excavations that have Hebrew writing including an image with the name of Moses and the Ten Commandments. Dating of these artifacts is around AD 600, a time, Dr. Meldrum notes, that corresponds to the Book of Mormon closing accounts.[99]

- The Book of Mormon documents the appearance of Christ in the Americas where the sun was blotted out at the time of the crucifixion of Jesus (3 *Nephi* 8:5-23). "And there could be no light, because of the darkness, neither candles, neither torches; neither could there be fire kindled . . . so there could not be any light at all." One LDS scholar, David Calderwood, recounts a pre-Columbian history as told by the Incan patriarchs. "...the land and provinces of Peru were dark and neither dark nor daylight existed." Also "...they did not see the sun and could light no fires." The story continues, "...shortly after the sun reappeared, a white man, Ticci Viracocha-- the creator of the world--appeared among the Indians and performed many miracles."[100]

- At the time of Christ's crucifixion, The Book of Mormon describes major geologic upheavals including swallowing of cities into water (3 Nephi 8:9-18). In the 1950's,

---

[99] See www.firmlds.org website. Also see Appendix H for some discussion relative to this.

[100] Calderwood (p.132-33) this a book extensively documenting Hebrew influence in the Early Americas. Joseph Smith had no access to these early recorded accounts (pre-Columbian) of the Incas (published after the publication of the *Book of Mormon*), telling of their early (pre-Columbian) history.

archeological finds in Mesoamerica note a series of cataclysmic events dating around the time of Jesus' crucifixion. These events resulted in the formation of lakes and other changes to the appearance of the region.[101]

- Societal studies of ancient Mesoamerica show a major shift in religious practices coinciding with the Book of Mormon description of Jesus' appearance in the Americas. For instance, there was an abandonment of figurine-cult practices and the burning of incense in Mesoamerica around the time of the crucifixion of Jesus. Suddenly giving up old established folk traditions could be explained by a religiously powerful event such as the appearance and teachings of Jesus as documented in the Book of Mormon.[102]

- The common belief In Joseph Smith's time regarding Native Americans was that there were probably unsophisticated "scattered bands"[103], on the American continent during the time of the Book of Mormon events.[104] However, the Book of Mormon describes large, sophisticated, populations (sometimes in the thousands) in the Americas long before Columbus' arrival. Recently

---

[101] Christensen, (p. 3-11).

[102] Paraphrased from Yorgason, Warren, & Brown, (p. 173).

[103] Mann, (Kindle location 1491).

[104] Mann, (Kindle location 448-495) describes the societal contributions to fallacies of thinking that led to this idea. Much of his book deals with further discussion around this.

scholars have documented Mesoamerican cities and towns as early as 1800 BC, including the archeological remains of several villages around Lake Titicaca in 800 BC.[105] Also a city (Chavin de Huantar) of several thousand people from 800 BC to AD 200.[106] At the time of Christ, there was a village at Lake Teccoco that, "over the next four centuries, may have reached 200,000 inhabitants.[107] In other words, the Book of Mormon is describing large organized populations that were deemed unimaginable in the 1800's when the book was written. Another, improbable idea if the book were written through man's imagination.

This is just a sample of the evidence and studies that are out there.[108] Given the difficulty identifying locations and the significant effects of the climate deteriorating artifacts (which can't be overstated) I am impressed with what has been discovered so far. I am really optimistic about what will yet be

---

[105] Mann, (Kindle location 629). Wikipedia documents major occupation as early as 1,200 BC with periods of decline over time.

[106] Mann, (Kindle location 4891).

[107] Mann, (Kindle location 2425). While there is disagreement regarding total numbers, it appears quite likely the number in Central Mexico exceeded the populations of Spain and France together at the time of Columbus. (Kindle location 1998-99). Earlier estimates are also stated. For example, (Kindle location 2425) notes an estimate of 200,000 inhabitants in a location at the time of Christ.

[108] Porter and Meldrum present strong arguments for North American locations but I am having difficulty verifying much their empirical data relative to most of the *Book of Mormon* years (better luck on the final years) and thus don't detail it here. See Appendix G for some further detail. See also Wright.

discovered. As you have probably noticed, this evidence is equal to, if not more substantial than Old and New Testament findings. More substantial because much of this confirmed information was not available at the time of the writing of the Book of Mormon, something that cannot, for the most part, be said for the Old and New Testaments. Combining the Book of Mormon evidence with the Old and New Testaments makes a very strong case in support of Judeo-Christian teachings and religious aspects of all of the documents.

Dear Dad,

Well, I have to say, there seems to be an awful lot of confirming information regarding the Book of Mormon.[109] So much for the critics who say there is none. How can they in honesty make their arguments knowing the Book of Mormon was clearly written before most of the supporting evidence was known? This seems "extraordinary" evidence for skeptics of good will. I guess, however, like you say, truth for any individual is the data paid attention to and the importance given to that data.

Son,

I agree with you but there is even more compelling evidence to support the Book of Mormon. Before I say more, I want to remind you the importance of a spiritual testimony. It is the only way to absolutely resolve these questions, and I think that is by divine design. Reading the scriptures themselves and being willing to attend to the spiritual urgings that result will build a testimony that empirical data can never match.

---

[109] I find the blog jefflindsay.com to be a very informative and balanced source of information regarding much of the empirical data related to the Book of Mormon validity.

That being said, however, there is a connected series of events I would like to review with you. In my opinion they are really exceptional and additionally compelling pieces of empirical data. So that the impact of the facts I present and have already presented, will be fully appreciated, I want to remind you of a conversation we had earlier. We talked about the idea of zeitgeist - referring to the spirit of the time - this is what influences contemporary cultural thought and creativity. When we see confirmed deviations from the spirit or theories of the time, it should cause an honest truth-seeker pay attention to what is happening. With that in mind, let's look at the accounts of the travels found in 1 Nephi 1-18. *The* Book of Mormon opens with an account of a prophet from Jerusalem, Lehi, who was a descendant of the ancient Biblical prophet Joseph. Interestingly, the name Lehi appears in the book of Judges in the Old Testament. The name appears in the tradition where Sampson, of the Old Testament, slew 1,000 Philistines with the jawbone of an ass; the Hebrew word for jawbone being Lehi.[110] There is some current speculation surrounding an excavated location outside of Jerusalem by the name of Horvat Beit Loya (alternate name Beth Lehi or Lei). This area was first surveyed in 1899 (almost 70 years after the publication of the Book of Mormon).[111] Work is underway to determine if this site actually refers to the Lehi of the

---

[110] Gutfeld & Haber (p. 10).

[111] Gutfeld & Haber (p. 5).

Book of Mormon.[112] However, Bedouin traditions relate an account of an ancient prophet from this area by the name of Lehi, dated around 600 B.C, who mysteriously disappeared.[113]

Now, getting back to the story, Lehi and his family, along with a man named Ishmael and his daughters, fled Jerusalem just before it was captured by Babylon. To play devil's advocate for a minute, let's assume Joseph Smith, or somebody at his time, decided to make up a story of this family migrating to the Americas. Pulling out a map available to Joseph Smith, there are two logical routes a fabricated story might follow. One, would be to have the family cross through the Bering Straits, harmonious with an unchallenged theory popular even at that time (although the time periods are later). The second would be to have the family disembark from the Mediterranean Sea, taking advantage of the shortest distance, trade winds, and currents. The Book of Mormon, however, details a dramatically different and a highly improbable route. The party traveled southward through Saudi Arabia to the shores of the Red Sea, perhaps following the silk and

---

[112] Allen & Allen quote Chadwick who stated, "Beit Lei has nothing to do with Lehi or the *Book of Mormon*. The name does not refer to Lehi or to the House of Lehi." My opinion is that there are some positives and some negatives yet to be resolved. Positives are I think it legitimate to link "Lehi" with Samson slaying the Philistines with a jawbone and the site existed at the time of Lehi. The reporting of the Bedouins further substantiates this. Negatives are the time has not been specifically linked to the "prophet" Lehi and I am not certain of the Bedouin testimony on the internet. One of my initial reactions was, "Is it being given to 'promote' the site to tourists? Conversation with some who have knowledge of the site and have visited several times, indicate the Bedouin tradition is long standing. If the negatives can be resolved, this is, in my opinion, a strong exhibit.

[113] Interview with a Bedouin Sheik, www.beitlehifoundation.org/videos/. UVU Beit Lehi Archeological Project video.

incense trade route at times. Remembering the zeitgeist influence, why would Joseph Smith do this if he were making it up and wanted a credible story?

It is my testimony that he was not making it up and these were actual events. Using information from the Lachish Letters[114] and hints in the scriptures, we can assume that the lives of Lehi's party were in danger from both government officials and others of influence. Therefore, perhaps they were led to travel this unexpected route to avoid being harmed.

After arriving at the Red Sea, they traveled three days in the wilderness (1 Nephi 2:4-6) and encamped in an area they called, "The Valley of Lemuel." As you know, Lemuel was the name of one of the sons of Lehi. They described high cliffs and a source of continually running water that emptied into the Red Sea. A current Internet article by a minister hostile to the Book of Mormon quotes the Arabian Desert as "bone dry" and labels this an impossible location. An internet search of "Valley of Lemuel," however, produces a description of Arabian Desert Wadi Tayyib AL-ISM with photographs of a valley with 2,000 foot sides and a stream, located three day's journey from the Red Sea; the proper direction and travel time stated in the Book of Mormon.[115] Again, information regarding this location was not available at the time to Joseph Smith and would be considered as merely fanciful.

Back to the story, the party continued a southerly direction. Along the way, Ishmael died. The Book of Mormon relates how they buried him in Nahom (1 Nephi 16:34). Nahom,

---

[114] See pp. 27-28 of this book for a brief description of the Lachish Letters.

[115] A somewhat detailed summary of the "accidental" discovery of the valley by his party with a stream through it is provided by Allen & Allen (p.514-16).

by the way, is similar to a prophet's name (not a geographical location) in the Old Testament probably having no relationship. In the 20th century French archeologists discovered many thousands of ancient burial tombs in a location compatible with the Book of Mormon account. They estimated burials occurred from about 3,000 BC to about AD 1,000. There they found the name Nahom (NHM) engraved on stone.[116] Critics point out exploration was done in the 1700's and a map of Arabia was generated which included numerous locations. One of them was Nahom.[117] It is unlikely Joseph Smith was aware of this map and there was no way for him to know it was a major burial site.

The narrative continues but again takes an illogical turn. As Lehi's group approaches the Arabian Sea, instead of disembarking at that point, as would be expected if the story were being fabricated, the party went inland, due east. This turn brought them through difficult desert conditions. Eventually they camped and built a vessel on the backside of a mountain range. This deviation from a logical and probable course was subject to disbelief and ridicule. There appeared to be no resources for

---

[116] Aston & Aston. A somewhat detailed account by the explorers themselves.

[117] Critics note a book by Christian Neibuhr, written in the 1700's was available in the library of a university close to Joseph Smith. Critics note the location for Nahom was listed in the book. I find maybe 50 within the diameter of a half dollar with names of places on the map by Neibuhr within any area around NHM. What is not mentioned by critics is the book is one of two volumes detailing Arab Life at that time. There are a myriad of other names along with Nahom and Nahom is not described as a major burial area. There has also been no indication Joseph Smith or any of his acquaintances at the time of the writing of the *Book of Mormon* had any interest or familiarity with ancient Arab culture and there is no indication they had any contact with this book or even knew of its existence (even if they had, the likelihood of choosing the name associated with massive burials is very improbable).

metal to make tools, sufficient trees to provide lumber, and no viable launch points for a boat from the backside of the mountains along Yemen and Oman onto the coast of the Arabian Sea. Utilizing the Book of Mormon accounts, 20th century exploration[118] discovered a location in Oman (Wadi Sayq/Khor Kharfor) where construction of a boat along with a viable launch point matches the Book of Mormon description. Also found was a metal source within a day's walking as well as an abundant food source.

The story continues. Having built a boat, Lehi's party set sail in the Arabian Sea, and ultimately arrived on the shores of the Americas. At Joseph Smith's time a trip from the Arabian Sea was considered not possible. The distances are great and the currents and winds are unfavorable to a continuous sailing venture. The complex nature of sailing from the Arabian Sea to the American continent remains a difficult journey even today. The Book of Mormon gives an account of a severe storm during sailing (1 Nephi 18:13-15). Some have speculated this storm drove the ship off course into more favorable currents. In addition, today, we understand the influences of a periodic weather event called El Nino that alters winds globally. This could also account for more favorable traveling conditions. Joseph Smith clearly did not know about this, but the Lord did.

As you know, the Book of Mormon continues with accounts of this group reaching the Americas. We have already discussed some of the changes in cultural practices as well as archeological findings that support the record that is in the Book of Mormon. Is there any rational person of good will who would consider this series of specific connected improbable events as coincidental? Or is it more likely confirmation of the Book of

---

[118] Aston & Aston (p. 19-20).

Mormon's divine origins? We are dealing with a significant amount, an exceptional amount, of strong logical evidence. In my opinion, we are well within the realm of providing the impressive extraordinary evidence required by skeptics. The information is clearly stated and increasing with ongoing research. To say it is insignificant denies the obvious.

CHAPTER V

SUMMARY

Dear Dad,

OK, as I see it, it looks like the Old and New Testaments are confirmed by geographical locations, events and names because there are a lot of them. Critics argue the religious stuff was made up to fit the already known locations and names. The same argument cannot be used with the Book of Mormon *because* there is so much specific, confirmed detail that was unknown at the time of Joseph Smith. I get it. I agree it is improbable, even impossible, that the Book of Mormon was made up. And, I would conclude, if the Book of Mormon was not made up, that means the much of the Old and New Testaments are true too. Thanks Dad. You've been a big help and support for me at this time.

Dear Son,

I'm glad this has been helpful to you. I had hoped it would be. Please indulge me just a few more minutes because the importance of the statements you just made are life changing and critical for your development and ultimate happiness. Because of my love for you, I want to emphasize what we have just been through. The reason I have spent so much time researching is because I wanted to make sure I had information that was honestly presented. There is much more detail I could have provided but I have tried to summarize points with minimum words and examples yet provide a fair representation of what is out there.

Stripping our earlier discussions down to the bottom line, we are left with several basic highly improbable points that are linked together in a unified account. Each point on its own exemplifies a high probability of verification. When these points are combined the probabilities magnify. The empirical evidence clearly supports the validity of the Book of Mormon and a person could not have written that it in the 19th (nor even the 20th) century.

I am aware that when faced with these points of evidence, the following arguments might be made:

- Chance. (Extremely unlikely due to a basic impossibility; not a logical conclusion).
- The Devil (Some specific religious groups' hypotheses at times, but not viable because the Book of Mormon provides strong testimony to the divinity of Christ and supports the validity of both the Old and New Testaments; not a Devil-like objective).
- External source - space aliens. (While unusual, there are those who honestly view this as a possibility. The Book of Mormon concerns itself exclusively to Christ. There is no mention of space aliens.
- The Book of Mormon is an external source, divinely inspired translation as Joseph Smith claimed.

The most reasonable conclusion is that last presented; the Book of Mormon is exactly what it says it is, another testament that Jesus is the Christ, a revelation from God. Today, more than ever, it is important to understand the validity of Judeo-Christian teachings. They are vital. Societies have depended upon them to remain humane. I am concerned that these teachings are no longer being widely honored and as you have discovered this year are, in fact, being ridiculed. Without future generations being taught these truths, how can our children learn truth from error? By accepting the principles taught in the scriptures we learn that

Jesus of Nazareth is the Messiah. With this knowledge come the comfort, guidance, and responsibility to adapt our lives accordingly. And, so, please consider the validity of the Book of Mormon establishes several facts:

- There is meaningful empirical evidence there is a God.
- There is meaningful empirical evidence God communicates with man in these times.
- There is meaningful empirical evidence there is a particular way God wants us to believe and conduct ourselves. Just being a generic good or self-satisfied person is a diversion that falls short of understanding the cogent issues.
- There is meaningful empirical evidence Jesus of Nazareth is the Messiah predicted in the Old Testament and described in the New Testament.
- There is meaningful empirical evidence Jesus of Nazareth existed and was resurrected.
- There is meaningful, empirical evidence Joseph Smith was a prophet.

All of these factors introduce a vital urgency for us in the way we think and act.

The Book of Mormon came about because a young man in the New England 1830's sought an answer from God as to which of the many various churches he should join. The answer was, in effect, "none of them". Further revelations restored the original and complete church of Jesus Christ (the Church of Jesus Christ of Latter-day Saints) and gave us the Book of Mormon as strong empirical evidence of a confirmation of Old Testament and New Testament claims. The Book of Mormon not only presents an empirically based, logical defense of God, Christ, and the Old and

New Testaments but also contains edifying and uplifting religious truths.

A spiritual, faith-based testimony is critical and necessary. I plead with you to read the scriptures and as you do so, keep an open mind and open heart asking God to let you know if what you are reading is true or not. For those of us whose spiritual testimonies are still developing, or are communicating with those who struggle, the Old and New Testaments, in concert with the Book of Mormon, constitute an empirically defendable case for the reality of the existence and claim of divinity for Jesus of Nazareth as the expected Messiah. Combined, these scriptures meet the "exceptional" criterion required by reasonable skeptics of good will. The Christian teachings and realities cannot be summarily dismissed; they are true, even by rational/empirical positions.

Since there is a God and there is a prescribed reason for us being here that relate to principles God has set into place, it is incumbent upon a reasoned mind to investigate what this purpose is and to start to seriously consider abiding by it; it has significant implications for how we conduct ourselves and the outcome of our future.

It is my belief... no, it is my knowledge that there is a specific reason we exist on earth at this time, that there is a God who interacts with us in our daily lives and there is a specific plan for our living to be in accordance with His guidance. While some aspects may be contrary to some of our natural desires, it all operates in our ultimate personal best interest. At this time we have all of the information, support systems and spiritual guidance we need. It should not be taken lightly. I know that Jesus of Nazareth is the predicted Messiah of the Old Testament and that the Old Testament, New Testament and Book of Mormon all refer to real religious events and contain vital information for our understanding and spiritual progress.

As a final note, I have continually referred to the importance of a spiritual testimony. An analogy that comes to mind is something I really enjoy, a fire in the fireplace. I enjoy the beauty of the sight and the warmth and gentle odor. From a distance it can be intellectually recognized, something anyone can do. It is most important, however that you get close enough to it and focus on it to feel it and appreciate the full reality. I sincerely hope that you will continue to examine these issues with an open mind and a sincere and open heart that you may also reach an assured knowledge of the truthfulness of these things; it is critical to you and your future. I have found it to be a life-long mission. Son, more than anything I wish for you to be sure in your testimony but it is something you must get for yourself. I encourage you to never give up your search for truth and to persevere through times like this when you feel your faith is shaky. And remember above all that I love you.

APPENDICES

APPENDIX A

Scholarly Interpretation of Paul's letters (p. 10 of text)

Doherty discredits the writings of Paul when they refer to the person of Jesus because of the use of the word "paralambo" ("Challenging the Verdict" p.62) referring to Paul's statement about his knowledge of Christ (Gal. 1:11-12). Doherty notes the word "paralambo" refers to passed on tradition or revelation, meaning the later. He states throughout, Paul uses the word "ophthe" meaning, was seen ("Jesus Puzzle" p.71). There is no evidence that he means anything more than a simple vision and this is borne out when Paul lists his own "seeing" with the rest. He makes no distinction between them. The Jesus Seminar, a group of diverse disciplines interested in the historical issues regarding Jesus, came to acknowledge that all these appearances are in the nature of "visions" and even this may be too strong a word. Doherty ("Challenging" 20-21) states the divine son referred to in Philippians 2:6 & 11 and Colossians 1:15-20 never equates the divine son to the human Jesus of the Gospels, but rather to a heavenly entity. In 1 Corinthians 15:3-7 Paul uses the term "received" implying he was told the events of Jesus' resurrection and appearances to others, yet in Galatians 1:11-12 he states he received his gospel from no man but from a revelation of Jesus Christ." Doherty notes the term, "receiving" was also used in pagan religious tradition to refer to the experiencing of a god's presence or revelation; a term used by Paul in both senses in the Galatians passage. Therefore, Doherty asserts Paul is saying he never received the gospel he preaches from any man, nor was he taught it but received it through a revelation of Jesus Christ.

Doherty concludes Paul, and others, are not referring to a person when they speak of Jesus but are reflecting reference to a divine spiritual level (more typical of Gnostics of the time)[119]

A brief example of a counter presentation is Jones (91-92) who takes a different view from Doherty regarding the meanings of the words of Paul in Cor. 1:18. Jones notes "paralambo," meaning "received" used in conjunction with "paradidomi," meaning "came from oral history," reflects upon Paul's visit to Jerusalem about 35 A.D. (Gal. 1-18) where he interviewed Peter (eyewitness) "historeo," personal investigation for the purpose of determining historical facts. Jones concludes the more accurate interpretations of the words are harmonious with Paul referring to an actual person.

---

[119] My summarization of conclusions by Doherty, CV, pp.183-184. Ehrman, p.7 &. Kimball, p.27 note the stronger political group of Roman Christians eventually labeled the "Gnostic Christians" (having fled massacre by the Roman armies into Egypt) as "heretics." Gnostic Christians appeared to have focused on the importance of the spirit and moved to a disdain for the physical, resulting in a position that Jesus did not actually possess a physical body.

APPENDIX B

Ways of Thinking (p. 11, 44 of text)

When we think about the human experience it is easy to define it such as the cognitive thinking as logical and the reaction to it as emotional. As long as we confine our experience into these two realms, we are missing a vital piece that has a much if not more validity and depth than these two areas of experience.

The important, even critical piece that is often overlooked is the spiritual experience that brings about change in our behaviors, our thought processes and our internal well-being. It is so important that the neglect of this portion of our being may explain the general malaise found in our current society.

The problem that I face as I write this is how to explain it to someone who has not recognized this portion of their experience. It reminds me of a time when I was explaining to a colorblind friend the various colors of a tattoo he had. He was patiently listening to my description when I suddenly realized, "these terms of color have no meaning to him". Sometimes it is just a matter of trying to tap into an almost experience and liken it to that. That is why we often describe the spiritual experience as being similar to how we feel when we are surrounded by the beauty of nature or see an exquisite piece of art. Similar, subjective experiences, but not quite there. It fact when we liken spiritual with nature or art we are really categorizing the spiritual with the emotional. I would assert that the spiritual for those who have experienced it and have developed a way of life around it would conclude that it is actually more logical than emotional.

This is so counterintuitive to those who have not experienced it that it will in fact sometimes lead to a reaction of scoffing or scorn. As I have read volumes of books from those who argue the spiritual points verses those who argue against it, I find it is often the case that both sides frequently end up being incredibly emotional in their response to the other. This is so clearly recognized when we begin to see the derogatory words such as, "cult, crazy, emotionally imbalanced, ignorant, racist, bigot, evil corrupt, stupid, etc.." While some of these terms have unbiased meaning, they can often flag strong emotional biases

An example of an emotionally driven comment is one made by Mark Twain something to the effect, " if Joseph Smith had left out the many instances of 'and it came to pass' from the Book of Mormon, the book would have been only a pamphlet." This, of course, is not true, [120] but it may be an emotionally motivated comment relative to one day when Mark Twain's father visited Brigham Young in Salt Lake City, Utah. Apparently Samuel (Mark Twain's actual first name) was misbehaving which irritated Brigham Young. Samuel had long hair and Brigham Young commented to Samuel's father, in front of Samuel, about his "daughter." Samuel, of course, took offense that probably generated his emotionally self-defensive antipathy for the Mormons, thus generating the "small pamphlet" comment as an adult. This incident also reminds me of the excessive amount of inflammatory antireligious statements made in Dawkins' book, *The God Delusion*. It strikes me that if all of the emotionally laden inflammatory content were omitted, his book would probably be just a pamphlet.

There is an excessive amount of emotionally generated criticism of the Book of Mormon, Joseph Smith, and other religious scriptures and characters through the use of derogatory terms, not infrequently by individuals who present themselves as operating from logical, unemotional stances. While some of these terms have unbiased meaning, they can often flag strong emotional biases.

It is my opinion the current world zeitgeist is caught up in a version of the emotional process; "If it feels good do it."

---

[120] See Donald W. Parry "And It Came To Pass" quoting *Roughing It*, Hartford, Conn: American Publishing Co. 1901. p. 133. Perry argues this phrase frequency appears in ancient Hebrew texts at a similarly high frequency, but not in the King James translation. This supports the ancient Hebrew of the *Book of Mormon* and separates it from a charge of sole dependence upon the *King James* translation.

Personal desires, urges, and impulses seem to take priority over restraint or moderation that is often advocated by religion. While tempting, a detailed discussion at this time is too far afield from our topic, so I will go no farther with it.

The cognitive model of human experience deals with information that is available to the sense of vision, taste, smell, touch, and hearing. Logical procedures have been devised to make this information meaningful by having rules. This is expressed in the scientific method of approach or in the legal approach. In the scientific model, data has to be able to be reproduced and controlled. In the legal model, scientific data is often used, but also there has to be a logical connection between points to arrive at a decision of "truth."

In this model, the simplest explanation with the fewest unsupported assumptions that are preferred for "truth." In the scientific model, it is always accepted that any given conclusion may be later modified be newly discovered data. This model can be experienced in conjunction with the emotional or physical as well as the spiritual. Some of the religious claims tend to be contrary to everyday experience, and are not the type of data that easily lends itself to the replication necessary to fit the scientific model of thinking. Therefore, for a person attempting to argue only on an empirical basis (even though they, however, may knowingly or unknowingly accept personal emotional influence) extraordinary evidence is required.

It is the logical procedures model that skeptics often focus on and require for acceptable inclusion under "truth." The spiritual model is required to be exhibited in the logical model before a skeptic accepts it. For some skeptics, there can be an emotionally protective barrier against allowing any manifestation of the spiritual in any way. However, for some, it is expressed in terms of "extraordinary claims require extraordinary proof."[121] It is an interesting side note that in American daily living, "proof beyond a reasonable doubt" is the standard. Skeptics drive the

---

[121] Carl Sagan, Wikipedia.

abnormal events into a range of proof that can only be provided by unexplainable events. One way this could be done is to provide observable data that is acknowledged to exist but can be explained in no other way other than the simpler explanation being a spiritual explanation.

When looking at the empirical approach to Christian accounts in terms of logical thinking, against the backdrop of the idea the stories were fabricated and did not relate to actual events, there are roughly three types of conditions:

1. The events in the accounts are all things that were common knowledge in the culture and could have been written at any time.

2. The events in the accounts provide some unique ideas that were not common in the culture of the time. Validity is indicated if these ideas are confirmed at a later time.

3. The events in the accounts provide not only unique ideas but, and this is very important, go against the common thinking of the time and are later confirmed. This condition, in order to be explained rationally, suggests ways of obtaining the information that are outside the reach of commonly accepted means.

Each condition might be looked at as an exercise in swimming. #1 is swimming in calm water; it is easily done. #2 is swimming against a slight current or with a current that is pushing sideways. It presents a challenge in that it takes considerably more effort than #1 but seems possible to do. #3 is swimming upstream, against a very strong current, and would take superhuman strength, exceptional conditions to accomplish.

I would suggest we look at the data related to Christianity and see how it goes in terms of what there is and what the simplest explanations for it are. It is my opinion, there are some strong evidences and the simplest explanations are in harmony with Christian beliefs.

APPENDIX C

New Testament Orthodoxy Issues (p. 15 of text)

Contemporary scholars[122] have stated, "Orthodoxy" in the sense of a unified group advocating an apostolic doctrine accepted by the majority of Christians everywhere, simply did not exist in the second and third centuries."[123]

For example, one position was expressed by Arius (300 A.D.) who "... was what we today would call a 'Bible fundamentalist,' ... because of his literal interpretation of Scriptures.

To Arius and his followers, God was completely transcendent, absolute, and indivisible. ... (his) main proof text from Scripture was Proverbs 8:22-31, ... 'The Lord begot me (Wisdom, Jesus) the firstborn of his ways'.[124] Jesus was created by God."

A contrasting opinion was expressed by Alexander (c300 AD.) who proclaimed that the Son was in all respects the equal to the Father, and also of the same substance or essence. Arius' insisted that the Son had been created by the Father, and therefore could not be co-eternal with His divine Parent; that the Son was the agent through whom the will of the Father was

---

[122] Eherman (p. 173) quotes Bauer, "Orthodoxy and Heresy in Early Christianity" as noting early (pre fourth century). As far back as we can trace our sources, could be found a number of divergent forms, none of which represented the clear and powerful majority of believers against all others. In some regions of ancient Christendom what became labeled as 'heresy' was, in fact, the earliest and principle form of Christianity."

[123] Ehrman (p. 173)

[124] Hill (p. 219)

executed, and that for this reason also the Son was Inferior to the Father both in nature and dignity. In like manner the Holy Ghost was inferior to the other members of the Godhead. A strong division within the Christian world resulted and Constantine, the Emperor, "Viewing himself as representing the divinity on earth and having God-given power over both material and spiritual matters, felt it his right to participate in the debates and to confirm the decisions made by the council."[125] The concluding debate resulted in a statement that is generally interpreted today that Jesus and God are of the same substance, the same being.

There was a problem in that the Greek word for "same substance" was, "... *homousios,* a slippery term that can be translated as 'one in essence', 'one in being,' or even 'same materiality.' The last two seem closer to what the council meant, but, for many, the ambiguity remained and the controversy was not closed. The decision by the council fathers to go beyond the Scriptures and to settle the Arian controversy through Greek philosophy was a crucial one. It represented a major adaptation of Christian belief to a perspective and culture other than that of the Scriptures. The three bishops who disagreed were deposed and

---

[125] Hill (p. 220).

banished from their cities by the emperor.[126] It appears the issue continues to the present day.[127]

It is my opinion one possible reason there is such conflict in people's minds over this issue, in part, goes back to the very first canonized scriptures. Genesis uses a plural noun when describing the creation, "Let us make man in our own image." The translation of this noun can mean two individuals or a committee of individuals. There did, however, appear to be a prevailing tendency of people to identify a number of gods in daily life, yet the Hebrews were consistently admonished to worship only one God, Jehovah, the creator (one of the creators) of this earth. When Jesus entered the scene, theologians were faced with developing a rational explanation of the apparent two Gods, e.g., "... whom thou hast given me, that they may be one, as we are." (John 17:1) and Jesus praying to His God (Matthew 26:3 & Luke 23:1). There was also the possibility of more than one god being associated with pagan beliefs.

Prior to Constantine, compounding the Christian experience, was occasionally aggressive persecution, particularly by the Roman government that included torture, killing, and destruction of records. In 300 A.D., Constantine came to power as

---

[126] Hill (p. 220), also presents more detail of the process and thinking by Constantine.

[127] David Knoll, an ordained minister co-pastoring a church in Wisconsin, authored a book, *Of the nature of the Father, Son and Spirit*. Pastor Knoll states, "Christian Theology teaches Jesus is also the one and only true God, is equal to the Father and has existed eternally with the Father, Son and Spirit ..." Suggesting a different perspective, Pastor Knoll states, "... the Bible never speaks of God the Son, God the Spirit, or the Father of God..." The Church of Jesus Christ of Latter-day Saints, views Jesus as God, (Jehovah) who is separate from His father, (Elohim) but of one mind and purpose. The Holy Ghost is also a separate entity but does not have physical form as God, the Father and Jesus, the Christ do.

the Roman Emperor and, for various and uncertain reasons (including the fact his mother was a Christian), he decreed Christianity to be the official religion of the land. Scholars note it became more desirable to be a member of the clergy than to be an officer in the Roman army. Constantine wanted to bring harmony to the realm that was being disrupted by serious clashes between Christians over doctrinal issues, primary of which was the difference of opinion on the nature or the Godhead. He ordered a council of religious representatives to convene in Nicaea to quickly forge an official statement of Christian creed so differences could be quieted. Of the 1,800 bishops who were invited, 300 attended. This process was described as involving considerable dispute and banning of some positions. Arius (God and Jesus were separate substances) was exiled along with two bishops who refused to endorse the position of Athanasius, a deacon to the Bishop of Alexandria (contending God and Jesus are same substance), and the leader of the opposition to Arius.[128] The historian Eusebius, "the father of ecclesiastical history", an ally of Aries, was not even invited to attend. Constantine made the final judgment in which parties were to be represented.[129] The dominant political force (and "winners" of the struggle) was

---

[128] Some contend (e.g. Ehrman) the process was heavily political and weighted in favor of the more powerful Roman Christians (Proto-Christians, a term coined by Ehrman, p. 222-223); others would contend God guided the process.

[129] Kimball & Stirland (p. 2-3).

considered by some scholars to be the Roman group (Proto-Christians).[130]

Out of this process came the Nicene Creed that is the basis for the current day core of Roman Catholic Church and many of the Protestant churches. Scholars note the victorious representatives to have sometimes altered the scriptures (later versions differed from earlier versions) to fit the Nicene definitions. One example, the original verses of Luke 3:22 quoted Psalms 2:7, "You are my Son, today I have begotten you" was changed to, "You are my beloved Son in whom I am well pleased."[131] While I don't consider such a change to be monumental, it does reflect, and is emphasized by critics, efforts by copyists to bring scriptural meaning more into line with the council decisions. Actually, the specific current theology of a God as being "... one only living and true God, everlasting, without body, parts or passions" was derived from 1646 A.D. Anglican Thirty-Nine Articles providing the basis for the formulations of the Presbyterians, Congregationalists, Baptists, and Methodists.[132]

---

[130] Ehrman, notes the Christian community in Rome was large and affluent. Rome was the capital of the Roman Empire. Roman Christians promoted a hierarchical structure insisting each separate unit only have one bishop. There was a judicious use of gifts offered to certain other churches with concomitant sympathetic hearing of their views. By the end of the 3rd century the Roman church was dominant (p. 175).

[131] Ehrman (p. 222-23).

[132] Terry & Fiona Givens, (Kindle location 1576).

APPENDIX D

The Apostasy (p. 17 of text)

Priesthood is the power and authority given to man to act in God's name for the salvation of His children. Through the priesthood we receive the ordinances of salvation as well as blessings of healing, comfort, and counsel.

During His mortal ministry, Jesus Christ established His Church with priesthood authority. It was led by prophets and apostles who taught correct doctrine and received revelation that was recorded as scripture. They also ordained others to carry the priesthood. With the death of the apostles, priesthood authority was lost from the earth, revelation ceased, and essential doctrines were lost or corrupted.

The Church of Jesus Christ of Latter-day Saints maintains through the Prophet Joseph Smith, the Church that Jesus Christ established was restored. Jesus Christ leads the Church today through apostles and prophets. These are righteous men who are called of God and given the priesthood

Priesthood authority was restored in 1829 when John the Baptist appeared to the Prophet Joseph Smith and Oliver Cowdery. He laid his hands on their heads and conferred on them the Aaronic Priesthood (see D&C 13). A short time later, Peter, James, and John of the original Twelve Apostles laid their hands on Joseph Smith and Oliver Cowdery and conferred upon them the Melchizedek Priesthood, which Peter, James, and John had received from Jesus Christ (see D&C 27:12–13).[133]

---

[133] See lds.org.

APPENDIX E

Old Testament Archeological Issues (p. 21 of text)

Wallace[134] noted in 1975 archeological excavation of the Ebla palace disclosed a library of writings dating from 2400-2300 BC These writings refer to the location of Canaan (reported to be doubted by some until then), the word "Tehom" from Genesis, the names Sodom and Gomorrah, the city of Haran and a creation account similar to Genesis. These discoveries provided confirming support for the Old Testament documents. Wallace also cites Nuzi, Mari and Bogazkoy clay tablets confirming the existence of the Hittites, the existence of Sargon's palace (Isaiah 20), the name Nabo-sharrussu-ukin linked to Nebuchadnezzar II (Jeremiah 39), a reconstructed wall (Nehemiah), discovery of the "City of David", and "... an example of an ancient king with an incredible concentration of wealth ... supporting Solomon's prosperity." The identification of previously unknown (outside of Old Testament mention) sites or names support the documents as legitimate sources of information thus supporting authenticity.

Regarding Sodom and Gomorra, apologist McDowell[135] states, "The destruction of Sodom and Gomorrah was thought to be spurious until evidence revealed that all five of the cities mentioned in the Bible were in fact centers of commerce in the area and were geographically situated as the scriptures describe." McDowell cites earthquake activity with, "bituminous pitch being hurled down on those cities that had rejected God ... Evidence of such burning has been found on the top of Jebel Usdum (Mount Sodom).

---

[134] Summary by Jim Wallace.

[135] McDowell (p. 95-95).

Wallace[136] also states, "The interesting fact is that the names of the Cities of the plain are spelled the same as they are in Scripture."He details several aspects of the area that parallel events described in Genesis. Wallace concludes reasons Bab edh-Dhra, because of size, was probably Sodo. "The other cities would follow Numeria = Gomorrah, Safi = Zoar, Feifa = Admah, Khanazir = Zeboiim" as possibilities.

Presenting a somewhat different perspective, you will find on Wikipedia "The historicity of Sodom and Gomorrah is still in dispute by archeologists, as little archaeological evidence has ever been found in the regions where they were supposedly situated. Archeologist Shaub stated Bab-edh-Dhra was destroyed around 2067 BC and Numeria at a different time period around 2600 BC. Several candidates are discussed including Tall el-Hammam that seems to fit the Bible descriptions of the lands of Sodom and disclosed an ash layer with human bone fragments (supporting the cataclysmic and sudden end consistent with the Bible account). Professor Eugene H. Merrill[137] is quoted, "... the identification of Tall el-Hamman with Sodom would require an unacceptable restructuring of the biblical chronology". Otherwise, archeological exploration is yet to provide further substantial empirical confirmation.

There is a recent posting on the internet[138] focusing on linguistic evidence demonstrating Jewish presence in ancient Egypt that eventually disappeared (suggesting they were there

---

[136] Wallace, web site

[137] Cited in the Wikipedia article.

[138] Jewish Journal article by Danielle Berrin reporting on a talk given by Gelit Dayon. See Berrin in Bibliography.

and then left). Cited was an Egyptian manuscript that described "plague is throughout the land ... blood is everywhere ... the river is blood ... and the hail smote every herd of field ... the land is without light and there is thick darkness throughout the land ... the Lord smote all the firstborn of Pharaoh in the land of Egypt-- from the first born sat on his throne to the firstborn of the captive who was in the prison..." Also cited were the names Moses ("an Egyptian name"), Pharaoh, the Red Sea/Sea of Reeds, Hebrews, Israelites,[139] and the presence of slaves in Egypt. Time frames were not indicated. Some scholars are unable to find evidence of the wandering of the Jews in Exodus and therefore have questioned the validity of it.

---

[139] Mykytiuk, (p. 42-50) lists 50 biblical personal names including David, who until 1993, had been considered by some critics as to be mythological that were confirmed by archeological finds.

APPENDIX F

The Shroud of Turin (p. 38 of text)

The Shroud of Turin is a large piece of fabric brought to light around the 14th century that has, over the years, been the subject of claims and counterclaims. The original tradition is that it is a burial cloth that covered the body of Jesus after he was crucified. An image of a face can be identified as well as markings corresponding to areas of wounds as would have been expected for Jesus after the crucifixion.

There has been considerable controversy, of course, over the authenticity of the shroud, including the reliability of reports of its history. A segment was carbon dated, placing it much later than the resurrection, around the 14th century. One of the counterclaims was the segment came from a later repair of the cloth, but this has been disputed. Also, it bears an image clear enough to see what Christ might have looked like. I will not go into detail as there is considerable back and forth information, too extensive for citation in this book. I will mention the issues include disputes whether stains are paint or blood, and whether the images are properly distorted to account for fabric position at the time of resurrection. I would like it to be true, as it would lend considerable support for the concept of a resurrection and I am attracted by the prospect of having a "photograph" of Jesus. However, I tend to be skeptical. I consider it "too good to be true." A quick search of video presentations on the Internet seems to produce mostly positive sides without the negative. I would recommend Wikipedia, T*he Shroud of Turin* and *Biblical Archaeology Society* (BAS) articles to get a more balanced (and ongoing) sense of the considerable claims and counterclaims. Needless to say many intelligent people have very strong feelings both ways on the authenticity and there is evidence supporting the various positions. This particular issue provides a good way to observe the concept that reality for any given individual depends upon the information attended to and the importance given that information.

APPENDIX G

Book of Mormon Issues (pp. 42, 49, 50, 58 of text)

View of the Hebrews

John Gee presents an analysis demonstrating only a remote similarity with the Book of Mormon and the *View of the Hebrews*. Gee notes there can be some points in common but also some important differences. For example some similarities are:

- Hebrew lineage. The Book of Mormon details three Hebrew groups that arrived on the American continent, the most recent around 600 BC. *View of the Hebrews* deals with the 10 Lost Tribes.
- The ability to construct large dirt mound fortifications.
- The presence of ancient Hebrew religious customs (extensive in *View of Hebrews*, vaguely alluded to and in considerably less detail in the Book of Mormon).
- The presence of decorative elements on shirts of religious leaders referred to by the author as representative of the Old Testament Urim and Thummim. Joseph Smith used Urim and Thummim stones to translate the Book of Mormon and also referred to in the Old Testament but the presence in clothing is not emphasized.

Gee lists several issues that distinguish the Book of Mormon from the *View of the Hebrews*, including:

- The narrative style of the Book of Mormon is in contrast to the analytical style of the *View of the Hebrews*.
- Gee stated, "In opposition to Ethan Smith, the Book of Mormon does not claim that all the American natives had one origin. In fact, the Book of Mormon reports at least

three different migrations from the Old World . . . and expressly allows that there were others..." p. 321.

- Ethan Smith argues that the original Native American language appears to have been Hebrew. Gee states, "Even though the language (of the Book of Mormon immigrants) may have been based on Hebrew... 'the Hebrew hath been altered by us also'" pp. 321-322.

- E. Smith argues that circumcision was widespread among the Native Americans. The Book of Mormon mentions it only once in a letter saying that the practice of circumcision has been 'done away.'

- E. Smith refers to 'dress and trinkets' and ceremonies while... the Book of Mormon does not describe the dress, and ceremonies are mentioned only obliquely and without detail.

- E. Smith claims that the Native Americans had a tribe like the Levites, and animals as signs of their tribes but the Book of Mormon has no such tribe as Levites and mentions no animals as emblems of tribes.

- E. Smith argues that the Native Americans had cities of refuge, but such cities are not mentioned at all in the Book of Mormon.

Narrative of Zosimus

A Kindle article in the *Deseret News*[140] provides a brief overview of a presentation Professor James Charlesworth of Princeton Theological Seminary. The topic of focus is a possibly first to third century Greek *Narrative of Zosimus* that may originally have been composed in Hebrew. The article quoted a

---

[140] Deseret News, *Defending the Faith: The Narrative of Zosimus and the Book of Mormon* Kindle edition, by Daniel Peterson. Apr. 9, 2015

summary of the document published by Welch noting similarities to, particularly, I Nephi in the Book of Mormon. An English version was not published until over 30 years after the Book of Mormon. The reason the *Narrative of Zosimus* has attracted attention are several similarities with the events in I Nephi. The story is about a righteous man (Zosimus) praying to the Lord and obtaining spiritual passage to a land of blessedness. Wandering in the wilderness, being transported (by branches of a tree) across an "unfathomable river" to a beautiful tree where he eats its fruit and drinks the "life sustaining water which flows from its roots." The party escaped from the destruction of Jerusalem at the time of Jeremiah, thus surviving "the scattering of Israel." The history is engraved on soft stone plates. The author concludes, "We can be virtually certain that Joseph Smith had never read –or heard of the *Narrative of Zosimus.*"

John W. Welch details a point-by-point comparison of *I Nephi and the* Narrative of Zosimus.[141] It is important to recognize Welch is speaking from a literary/cultural similarity between the two documents. I agree with the position that both have common cultural elements, particularly in the "dreams" or "visions" of Lehi. This type of analysis reminds me of the projective personality analysis techniques such as the Rorschach used by clinical psychologists. A stimulus is provided that carries the potential for ambiguity and the description provided by the person responding is strongly dependent upon personal experiences and motivations, cherry-picking of a sort. I say this, not to discredit stylistic analysis but to caution against trying to infer genesis of one from the other. Just briefly, there are considerable differences if one is approaching the issue of one of the manuscripts being the source of the other. If most would read *The*

---

[141] Welch, John, *Narrative of Zosimus*, p. 323-374.

Narrative of Zosimus without the motive of trying to find similarities, a conclusion of one being derived from the other would be an unlikely conclusion. I mention this article because it has similar potential for the same use that has been done with the *Spaulding Manuscript* and *View of the Hebrews.* I imagine there will be more of this as time goes on. When, however, the Book of Mormon is considered in the totality of evidence, it is apparent these stories are anomalies carrying some similarity but not coming close to providing alternative hypotheses of authorship.

DNA

There has been some discussion related to DNA and the Book of Mormon. I will summarize very briefly.

Porter and Meldrum discuss in some detail the existence of a mitochondrial DNA Haplogroup X subgroup noted in ancient American Natives but is not found in Asian strains. The specific subgroup of Haplogroup X is described as characteristic of Eastern European (in this specific case, Jewish) lines and is not found in those areas related to a Bering Strait migration. As intriguing as this presentation is, Haplogroup X is potentially contaminated with other Asian strains and, while remaining an active and lively discussion point, unfortunately is not supported by the opinions of experts at this time as either refutation or confirmation of the Book of Mormon.[142]

---

[142] Personal communication with Dr. John Butler (LDS geneticist) of National Institute of Standards and Technology (NIST) in 2014 indicates the genetic composition of the natives of the Americas are so contaminated and uncertain as to composition that, while there may be some Hebrew mixture, it currently cannot be related to the *Book of Mormon* at this time.

Mesoamerican/North American Issues

These authors, Porter and Meldrum, also advocate for a location of Book of Mormon events in North America (in contrast to Mesoamerica). Some of the empirical evidences the authors provide are metal helmets and breastplates, metal swords, military fortifications, and large population numbers with the Hopewell Indians whose time frame paralleled some of the Book of Mormon events. I have had difficulty finding empirical support for this position, in part because of an apparent insurmountable time difference between the ancient Hopewells and the technology necessary at the time. The location of Book of Mormon events seems to have become, for some, a point of strongly contested positions. Some of the North American advocates contend the Mesoamerican advocates lack spiritual orientation while some of the Mesoamerican advocates contend the North American advocates are ignoring facts.

While I have not yet taken the time to fully explore these positions, from the data I do have, it appears there is potential for some harmony between the two positions. In fact, there are several scenarios that are harmonious.[143] Thinking I tend to personally embrace is that, while the Book of Mormon people were among and sometimes intermixing with an already existing larger population, there could have been a select group who were maintaining a genetic identity. This group could have traveled with Moroni following the battle in the Mesoamerican Cumorah as they fled, carrying the plates of the Book of Mormon, further north culminating in the New York area. This is even compatible

---

[143] Wright presents a detailed discussion dealing with the "Heartland" (United States) and Mesoamerica issues, providing much discussion on a harmonious North-Mesoamerica combination likelihood.

with, if I interpret it correctly, a time line for an initial weak showing of the mtDNA Haplogroup X (3%) and increasing (50% in a select group)[144] within the time frame Moroni could have left the Cumorah defeat and migrated to North America. There appears to have been ample time for this to happen, if my take on the timelines is correct.

This is also compatible with Meldrum's discussion of Hopewell Hebrew findings dating to around AD 600, the closing period of the Book of Mormon.[145] It is also my opinion some of the wording conflicts are eased if it is kept in mind, at the time of the Book of Mormon events, there was no United States, no North America, no South America. There was just a block of land that eventually became titled the Americas with later designations of North, South, and Meso.

Of a more tangential note is the issue of a vision some associates with Joseph smith experienced in New York of a large cave with extensive plates and other artifacts. It is my opinion; this was a vision disclosing the original cave in the Mesoamerican Hill Cumorah. Moroni later carried and deposited in New York a selected grouping of the plates and artifacts of his people.

[144] Meldrum's reporting.

[145] See The FIRM Foundation (Foundation for Indigenous Research) website sponsored by Meldrum at www.irmlds.org.

APPENDIX H

Thinking of the Times, Zeitgeist (p. 29, 56 of text)

Let me back up a little to help get an understanding of a broader perspective on what is going on when we talk about the word zeitgeist. Every society has imbedded within it certain assumptions about the world – "Zeitgeist"[146] – that remain largely unchallenged. These assumptions, or beliefs, lead to certain inevitable intellectual, and moral and ethical convictions. These, in large part, define what the center is for any given society. In other words, they form the foundational basis for decision-making and moral judgment within that society. In the Unites States, the belief in the existence of God, in particular a God that interacts in peoples' lives, the Judeo-Christian God, has formed the backbone of the "Western" legal and social perspective. American society at one time simply and unquestionably accepted the notion that God exists, however that seems to be a diminishing central belief. An increasing number of individuals within the mainstream of American culture are drifting away from America's historically Judeo-Christian frame of reference. Interestingly, there seem to be a large number who don't even realize it. This drift manifests itself not only as a personal rejection of the Judeo-Christian concept of God by many, but of openly attacking Judeo-Christian concepts, beliefs, and values by some; even to the point of outright suppression of these beliefs. The emerging zeitgeist of our current times is to not only being skeptical of Christian beliefs but, increasingly, to be openly hostile.

---

[146] Boring detailed this phenomenon, labeling it with the German term "Zeitgeist" (spirit of the times).

To me, and too many other Christians as well, inspired faith is a potent, legitimate and viable reality. It is not blind, and does not need empirical validation. Religious skeptics, however, do not generally share this viewpoint. Rather than faith, which they consider to be unreasoned, unscientific, and baseless, they are persuaded only by empirical reproducible and/or provable or logical evidence. Ironically, many Christians, as well as religious skeptics, do not realize that a considerable amount of empirical or cognitively rational evidence actually exists. As such, they never even enter into a discussion about these matters.

APPENDIX I

Validity of Joseph Smith's Experience (p. 47 in text)

Briefly, the Book of Mormon came about in early 19th century Vermont. An uneducated (but intellectually capable and spiritually serious) teenage farm boy, Joseph Smith, was confused by the variety of religions that were contending against each other. Smith sincerely believed in God and knelt in prayer asking for guidance in which church to join. He had a vision in which he reported God, the Father and Jesus, the Christ appeared to him instructing him not to join any of the groups because, while they all had some truths, they also contained misleading errors. Eventually, Joseph Smith was guided to some ancient metal plates (no longer available today) that he translated through a revelatory process. The book was given the name, Book of Mormon, after one of the major figures in the book and a church, the Church of Jesus Christ of Latter-day Saints, was founded in 1830.

The Book of Mormon describes the events of at least 3 groups of Hebrews in the Jerusalem area migrating to the American continent[147] between 1,000 BC and 600 BC. While many strongly accept the Book of Mormon, there is also strong opposition from others. Some just do not know what to make of it. At Joseph Smith's time, and currently, people who are uncomfortable with it try to find alternative explanations that

---

[147] There is not universal agreement on which American continent(s) are being referenced in the *Book of Mormon*. Norman (2008), and Allen and Allen (2008), for example, argue in favor of the Mesoamerican area while Porter and Meldrum 2009) argue the United States of America. In terms of which continent (North or South American) the *Book of Mormon* covers, I think it may be possible to argue both. Resolution of this issue is yet to be determined although I tend to favor the Mesoamerican position.

were different from Joseph Smith's claim he translated the book by revelation.

Why would anybody care? The Book of Mormon entered into religious areas and the origin and nature, while in some ways in keeping with traditional Judeo-Christian ideas, was very different, even clashing with some universally accepted traditional concepts, from the culture at the time. Even people of faith questioned the viability of the claims the Book of Mormon was derived through a revelatory process from God. As might be expected, people with a strong motivation to reject Joseph Smith's experiences as genuine, devised explanations to discount it.[148] Such things as "fraud" and "psychosis or other mental aberrations," the questioning of the actual existence of the plates (seems more later than at the time of Joseph Smith), were popular. These were ideas I once subscribed to and would like to answer here but it would be getting somewhat askew of our purpose and I will resist. Just let me say, when I first began to evaluate the challenges, I found these allegations are not sustainable when the data is evaluated. In fact, when examining these issues, the data, viewed in total, strongly substantiates the validity of Joseph Smith's claims. The resulting Book of Mormon provides strong additional evidence and testimony of the reality

---

[148] I found critics offered hypotheses of seizure activity or deliberate fabrication (my personal investigations included psychotic hallucinations as a possibility) as explanations for the visions. I consider it beyond the scope of this discussion to go into the details of this but let me state that as a psychologist; I examined these issues very early in my church membership. Psychotic events and seizure activity can be easily dismissed as viable hypotheses; there is no solid data supporting them. The likelihood of attempts of fraudulent fabrication is another angle I pursued. In a nutshell, this can be easily dispensed of as well, in fact, when all the data are considered, a stronger confirmation of genuineness emerges.

of Jesus of Nazareth as the prophesied Messiah and that He was resurrected.

Another charge was that three of the key participants in the early formation of the Church, Oliver Cowdery, Martin Harris, and David Whitmer at one time, because of personal reasons involving pride, anger, and hurt feelings, left the Church. Some of them even experienced detailed visions with Joseph Smith. Critics contended this was evidence their testimonies were not genuine. Examination, however, of the lives of these men, disclose they never denied, and always reaffirmed, the experiences they reported. One even made it a point on his deathbed to reaffirm that the experiences he reported were genuine. Two of the three re-joined the Church at a later time. What appears to be a disavowal when some of data is looked at turns out to be avowal when all of the data is concerned. The fact they had personal differences of such a strong nature and continued to affirm their experiences, in fact, lends strong credibility to their claims.

APPENDIX J

Complexity in Name Analysis (p. 39, 47 in text)

I briefly mention the following merely to give an example of the difficulty of being very definitive relative to the analysis of ancient names. Characteristic of the complexity of comments made regarding names, one author, Hugh Nibley, noted the *Lachish Letters* (about 600 BC) included the name, "Mattanyahu", appearing at Elephantine as "Mtn" (writing without vowels was a characterization of early Hebrew). The Book of Mormon, interestingly, has the names of both Mathonihah and Mathoni. Also, "the Book of Mormon has both long and short forms in the names of Amalickiah, Amaleki, and Amalici" (Elephantine MLKih). Apparently the interpretation and comparison of names is somewhat of a murky issue and there was another author taking exception with some of this interpretation.[149] Ricks[150] notes the or-ns and proper names characteristic of the Israelite and Egyptian background are characteristic of the or-ns and proper names used in the Book of Mormon.

There are issues with proper names that are present in the Book of Mormon but were not commonly known at the time it was written, again going against the zeitgeist. The translation issues of names are complicated with a lot of gray zones and need to be looked at in relationship to other information. If other information supports the interpretations given the names, the greater the validity.

---

[149] Internet article by Thomas J. Finley, protestant biblical scholar.

[150] See Ricks (p. 399-406)

BIBLIOGRAPHY

Ahmad, Hazrat Ghulam. *Jesus in India*. Islam International
    Publication LTD, 1989. Reproduced on Web.
    www.geocities.com/athens/delphi/1340/jesus_in_india.html

Alexandre, Yardenna, brief article from the ARCHEOLOGY Archive
    vol. 63, Number 2 March/April 2010 on Web.
    (www.archeology.org)

Allen, Joseph Lovell and Blake Joseph Allen. *Exploring the Lands of
    the Book of Mormon, Second Edition.* Orem, Utah: Book of
    Mormon Tours and Research Institute, LLC, 2008.

Ammon Ben-Tor, BAR 39:04 Jul/Aug 2013

Anderson, Russell. Web "The Spaulding Theory Debunked."
    http://www.lightplanet.com. . 10/04/06

Aston, Warren P. "The Rings That Bound the Gold Plates."
    Meridian Magazine, Kindle, 27 Nov. 2010:

Aston, Warren P. and Michaela Knoth Aston. *In the Footsteps of
    Lehi*. Salt Lake City, Utah: Deseret Book Company, 1994. Print.

ben Yehoshua, Hayyim *Refuting Missionaries*, on Web
    mama.indstate.edu/user/nizrael/jesusrefutation.html 2005.

Berrin, Danielle. "'Passover proof lies in Egyptian hieroglyphics' by
    Egyptologist Gelit Dayon." *Jewish Journal*, 12 Nov. 2014. Web.
    2015 Internet posting discussing 2010 presentation.

Calderwood, David G. *Voices from the Dust, New Insights Into
    Ancient America.* Austin, Texas: Historical Publications, Inc.,
    2005. Print.

Christensen, B. Keith. *Foretold and Found, Ancient America and
    Predicted Evidence of the Book of Mormon*. Provo, Utah:
    Centaur Print Partners, 2007. Print.

Doherty, Earl. *Challenging the Verdict.* Ottawa, Canada: Age of
    Reason Publications, 2001. Print.

Doherty, Earl. *The Jesus Puzzle, Canadian Humanist Publications.* Ottawa, Ontario: *Age of Reason Publications,* 1999. Print.

Ehrman, Bart D. *Lost Christianities* New York, New York; Oxford University Press, Inc. 2003. Print

Finegan, Jack. *The Archeology of the New Testament.* New Jersey: Princeton University Press, 1992. Print.

Fredricksen, Paula. *From Jesus to Christ.* New Haven and London: Yale University Press, 2000. Print.

Funk, Robert W. *The Jesus Seminar: The Gospel of Jesus.* Santa Rosa, California: Polebridge Press, 1999 Print.

Gee, John. *The Wrong Type of Book in Echoes and Evidences of the Book of Mormon.* The Foundation for Ancient Research and Mormon Studies (FARMS), Provo, Utah: Brigham Young University, 2002. Pp. 307-320. Print.

Givens, Terry I. and Fiona. *The Crucible of Doubt.* Salt Lake City, Utah: Deseret Book Company, 2014. Print.

Gjorgjiveski, Borce *History of Western Magick* www.geocities.com/nisetar/history.html. 2008

Gonza'lez, Justo L. *The Story of Christianity Volume 2.* New York: Harper Collins Publishers, 1985. Print.

Gutfeld, Oren and Michal Haber. *A guide to Beit Loya (Lehi): An Archeological Site in the Judean Lowland.* Jerusalem: Beit Lehi Foundation, 2009. Print.

Hall, Harriet. "Philosophy Meets Medicine (book review)." *Skeptical Enquirer* Vol. 38 No. 1 (January/February 2014): 53. Committee for Skeptical Inquiry. Amherst, NY.

Hill, Brennan. *Jesus the Christ, Contemporary Perspectives.* Mystic, Connecticut: Twenty-Third Publications, 1992.

Hilton, John L. *The Evidence of Ancient Origins.* Provo, UT: Foundation for Ancient Research and Mormon Studies: 2010

Johnson, Ludwell H. "Men and Elephants in America." *The Scientific Monthly* (1950). 77.

Johnsen, Stephen F. *The Empirical Jesus of Nazareth*. Unpublished organized notes summarizing a large number of references relating both to pro and con arguments. 2013.

Jones, Timothy Paul. *Misquoting Truth*. Downer's Grove, Illinois: Inter Varsity Press. 2007.

Kimball, Glenn. *Hidden Stories of the Childhood of Jesus*. Lawrenceville, Georgia: BFPublishing. 1997.

Kimball, Glenn, and David Stirland. *Hidden Politics of the Crucifixion*. Salt Lake City, UT: Ancient Manuscript Publishing. 1998.

Knoll, David. *The God of Jesus: A Comprehensive Examination of the Nature of the Father, Son and Spirit*. Indiana: West Bowl Press. 2012.

Koster, John P. *The Atheist Syndrome*. Brentwood, Tennessee: Woemuth & Hyatt, Publishers, Inc. 1989.

Madsen, Truman G. *Ultimate Questions*. Gazelman Foundation (distributed by Deseret Publishing). 2014. DVD.

Magee, M.D. "Other Miracle Workers." *Askwhy.co.uk/Christianity*. Contents updated Monday, November 23, 1998. http://www.askwhy.co.uk/christianity/0740Apollonius.html.

Mann, Charles C. *1491: New Revelations of the Americas Before Columbus*. 2nd ed. New York: Random House. 2005.

McDowell, Josh. *The New Evidence that Demands a Verdict*. Nashville: Thomas Welsch Publications. 1999.

Metcalfe, Brent Lee. Ed. *New Approaches to the Book of Mormon*. Salt Lake City, Utah: Signature Books. 1993.

Muncaster, Ralph O. *Can Archaeology Prove the New Testament?* Eugene, Oregon: Harvest House Publishers. 2000.

Mykytiuk, Lawrence. "Did Jesus Exist? Search for Evidence Beyond the Bible." *Biblical Archeology Review* 40.2 (2015): Pages. Web. 08 Dec. 2014.

Neibuhr, Christian. *Travels Through Arabia and Other Countries in the East.* Edinburg: Herron Rtr. 1792.

Nibley, Hugh W. *Dark Days in Jerusalem: The Lachish Letters and the Book of Mormon:* Provo, Utah: Maxwell Institute. Reprint. See also internet article, *The Lachish Letters: Documents from Lehi's Day,* www.lds.org/ensign/1981/12/lachish-letters-document-from-Lehis-day? Dec. 1981.

Norman, Garth. *Book of Mormon - Mesoamerican Geography: History Study Map.* American Fork, Utah: ARCON, Inc. 2008.

Parry, Donald W., and Ricks, Stephen D. *The Dead Sea Scrolls.* Provo, Utah: Foundation for Ancient Research and Mormon Studies (FARMS). 2000.

Persuitte, David. *Joseph Smith and the Origin of the Book of Mormon.* 2nd ed. Jefferson, NC: McFarland & Company, Inc. 2000.

Porter, Bruch H., and Rod L. Mehldrum. *Prophecies and Promises: The Book of Mormon and the United States of America.* Salt Lake City, UT: Digital Legend Press and Publishing. 2009.

Reynolds, Noel B. *Book of Mormon Authorship Revisited: The Evidence for Ancient Origins.* Provo, Utah: Foundation for Ancient Research and Mormon Studies. 1997.

Ricks, Stephen D. "Converging Paths: Language and Cultural Notes on the Ancient Near Eastern Background of the Book of Mormon." In *Echoes and Evidences of the Book of Mormon,* 389–419. Provo, Utah: FARMS. 2002.

S, Acharya [D.M. Murdock]. *The Christ* Conspiracy. Kempton, Illinois: Adventures Unlimited Press, 1999. Print.

Salopekm, Paul, and John Stanmeyer. "The Wells of Memory."
    National Geographic July, 2014: 85-86. Washington, DC:
    National Geographic Society.

Smith, D. Moody. "John – Historian or Theologian?" In *Biblical
    Archaeology Society* 20.1 (Oct. 2004): 22-31, 45. Print.

Smith, Ethan. *View of the Hebrews 1825: Or the Tribes of Israel in
    America.* Colfax, WI: Hayriver Press. 2002.

Sorenson, John L. *An Ancient American Setting for the Book of
    Mormon.* Salt Lake City, UT: Deseret Book Co. 1985. As cited
    by Fair Mormon, 283. Provo, UT: FARMS. 1996.

Strobel, Lee. *The Case for Christ.* Grand Rapids, MI: Zondervan
    Publishing House. 1998.

Tipler, Frank J. The *Physics of Christianity.* New York: Doubleday
    Publishing. 2007.

Tvedtnes, John A. *Ancient texts in support of the Book of Mormon
    in Echoes and Evidences of the Book of Mormon.* 231-260.
    Provo, UT: FARMS. 2002.

Urlaub, Cristofer Nobel. *Philosophies of Men Mingled with
    Scripture* (Blog). 2011.

Wallace, J. Warner. "Cold Case Christianity." *J. Warner Wallace –
    Cold Case Christianity.* http://coldcasechristianity.com

Welch, John. "Chiasmus and the Book of Mormon." *New Era.* Salt
    Lake City, UT: The Church of Jesus Christ of Latter-day Saints.
    February 1972.

Welch, John. *The Narrative of Zosimus (History of the Rechibates)
    and the Book of Mormon,* in *Book of Mormon Authorship
    Revisited, The Evidence for Ancient Origins,* Chapter 13,
    Foundation for Ancient Research and Mormon Studies, Provo,
    Utah 1997

Wirth, Diane E. *A Challenge to the Critics.* Bountiful, UT: Horizon
    Publishers. 1986.

Wright, Mark Allen. "Heartland as Hinterland: The Mesoamerican Core and North American Periphery of Book of Mormon Geography." *Heartland as Hinterland*. 2013. Conference, August 1, 2013.

Yorgason, B.B., B.W. Warren, and H. Brown. *New Evidences of Christ in Ancient America*. Arlington, VA: Stratford Books. 1999.

INDEX

Z

56974897R00082

Made in the USA
Charleston, SC
02 June 2016